For Seminar info contact:
The Gentry Agency
Alana Gentry
800-640-0848
alana@rickbrinkman.com
www.rickbrinkman.com
dr.rick@rickbrinkman.com

Love Thy Customer

Love Thy Customer

 *Creating Delight,
Preventing Dissatisfaction,
and Pleasing Your
Hardest-to-Please
Customers*

Dr. Rick Brinkman and
Dr. Rick Kirschner

McGRAW-HILL

New York | Chicago | San Francisco | Lisbon
London | Madrid | Mexico City | Milan | New Delhi
San Juan | Seoul | Singapore | Sydney | Toronto

1 2 3 4 5 6 7 8 9 0   DOC/DOC   0 9 8 7 6 5

ISBN 0-07-144802-0

This book is printed on recycled, acid-free paper containing a minimum of 50% recycled, de-inked fiber.

Contents

How Do I Love Thee

How do I love thee?
Let me count the ways.
I love thee during working hours
In the hope of simpler days

I honor thee when counting cost
Of trouble gained, referral lost
I love thee at the center of
All thoughts and actions, choices too

I help thee in thy painful hour
I care for thee with helping heart
With cooling words and warming smile

I teach thee when thy need is great
For learning all our ways
If failing that, I know t'would be
My business gone if not for thee

To do no harm, and harm undo
I help thee to relieve thy stress

In reaching for my true success
I honor thee and speak for thee
Lest my business fall to worthlessness

How do I love me?
Let me count the ways.
I love thee every time we meet
And dream of better days

When time is waste, your clouded face
I love thee more for loving's sake

Of rough commands, and heated wrath
Reaction shunned and traction gained

I spring to action strong and fast
Divide the present from the past
When heat is hot, emotions flare
'Til clarity is brought to bear
I shall attend thee and show I care

Should mouth be open
And mind be closed
I bend my knee to not oppose
Both your manner and your prose

Love Thy Customer

Or hopeless now, thy whining great
My questions draw forth into light
And then remove the weight

If words like arrows lack remorse
Then I remove them
Seek the source

Decisions made, yet still delayed
Some this, some that, and yet I serve
With gentle voice and plans to trade

A paradox to find this sign
No words express thy feelings deep
I speak for thee, and thus reveal
The time is long, no moment cheap

Relationship's a fickle thing
So I love thee as I love myself
A golden rule for truth to tell
'Tis you I live to serve so well

PART ONE
TRUE LOVE

Honor Thy Customer

How do I love thee? Let me count the ways.
I love thee during working hours
In the hope of simpler days

You may be working in a place that fields hundreds of incoming calls each day or sees a lot of foot traffic moving through the aisles and past the registers. Maybe your job is mining the rich field of sales possibilities, or you were hired and trained to answer complicated technical questions. Or maybe your Customers are patients, and your job is to deal with serious life-or-death issues. When you answer the call to service, that which you serve bestows an opportunity for fulfillment on your life. And in that moment, it all comes down to you. Giving the best possible service in that moment is exactly what this book is about.

In this context, what is love? Love is a relationship based in, built on, nurtured by, and developed through service. When some people hear the word *love*, they immediately think of romance. Yet the truth of love is more expansive than that. Love of nature. Love of country. Love of God. Brotherly love. Unconditional love. Some say that all you need is love because at both the beginning and end of life, love is all there is. So why should you bring love into your work?

Because without the principles of love to guide you, relationships grow complicated, people turn sour, and communication becomes progressively more difficult and nonproductive—painful even. Serve with love—love of anything—and you find fulfillment. Fulfillment gives life dignity and meaning. And so it is an honor to serve.

"You're gonna have to serve somebody."
—BOB DYLAN

What are the principles of love that allow you to honor thy Customer and serve well? Understanding. Connection. Healing. Education. Improvement. Advocacy. Support.

Perhaps your service is to a greater good, or to a principle, or to a future rich with promise. Perhaps your service is given in service to your family, your community, your country, or the world itself. In every case, when you learn and apply the principles of love for your Customer, you gain many valuable and important benefits in return. Relationships with Customers can be challenging and stressful. But these principles can help you to simplify your work and prevent many of the complications that make work unpleasant and overwhelming, to become an essential member of your service team, to build a solid track record of effectiveness that makes you more valuable to your organization now and into the foreseeable future, and to make each day more enjoyable than it would be without them. The principles of love will help you to feel vital and alive, give purpose and clarity to the work you do, and provide more joy and fulfillment in the relationships you cultivate with Customers.

These first few pages are only the beginning of your relationship with us and our service to you. Yet we feel confident in telling you, on behalf of the many people you will serve over the course of your lifetime, that you have our love and gratitude for honoring, caring, learning, teaching, speaking for, and, yes, loving your Customers.

CHAPTER 1

Understand Thy Customer

I honor thee when counting cost
Of trouble gained, referral lost

As Mary walked into the office, the first thing she noticed was disarray. A pile of paper here, a pile of folders there, a file drawer open, a napkin under a chair. "I sure hope they aren't as sloppy with my health care!" she said to no one in particular.

The receptionist seemed more interested in her computer. Every second that Mary stood there waiting seemed like an eternity, and she had the fleeting thought of making a break for it.

Her escape fantasy was shattered by a curt, "Yes?" Mary turned to see the receptionist's face as it formed an expression that seemed to say, "Well, what do you want? I'm waiting!"

"I am Mary Stern, and I am here for my appointment."

The receptionist returned her attention to her computer and in what appeared to be an afterthought said, "Take a seat. We're a little behind."

Mary asked, "How far behind?"

"It's hard to say" was the receptionist's perfunctory reply.

Mary fretted aloud, "I'm sorry, but I have another appointment after this one, and it's across town, and well, you know how the traffic is."

Without looking up, the receptionist simply said, "Take a seat. We'll get to you."

Mary sat down, her mind now racing. "I may have made a mistake in coming here, but if I cancel now, no doubt these jerks will charge me for it!" A half hour later, she still sat there, fuming. ❧

Perception Is Everything

All your relationships with Customers are threads of moments of truth that weave the fabric of what will be. Do you know what a moment of truth is? It is any moment that makes an impression. From the moment in which you greet people, whether in person or on the phone, to the moment they tell you their needs, concerns, or problems, to the moment when you respond to what they've told you, to the moment when a transaction is complete, your Customers are forming ideas and drawing conclusions about you, your organization, and the quality of service they are receiving. And in those moments, either you are adding love to or subtracting love from the relationship, simplifying the next moment or growing the complexity of what is required of you. Ironically, though, your relationship with your Customers is not about reality. Relationships revolve, devolve, or evolve around perception.

Whose perception? Your Customer's! You can think you're winning and be losing or think you're losing and be winning big. You can think you're doing everything right while everything is going wrong, and you can believe you're saying and doing all the wrong things, only to find that your Customer is grateful for your exceptional service. If you intend to Love Thy Customer, it is your Customer's perception that counts. It is amazing how a Customer's perception of service in these moments of truth has such a dramatic impact on Customer behavior. And negative moments make a much more lasting impression than positive ones! This is why we say that perception is all there is!

Little Counts Big

Customers, like all people, are quick to generalize. And once a generalization is formed, Customers, like all people, begin to look for evidence and proof. Generalizations can work for you or against you. And it boils down to moments of truth that make an impression on Customer perception, where it's the little things that count big! Rather than the latest and greatest whiz bang value-added feature or benefit, the heart and soul of Customer delight is derived from the little things. It is ironic how little it takes to delight your Customer!

In every moment of truth, your Customer is gathering perceptions that all too quickly become his generalization about you and your organization. If treatment generally is better than expected when your Customer interacts with you, that Customer is going to generalize positively, and inevitable mistakes and problems will be explained away or ignored. If, on the other hand, the treatment your Customer receives is mediocre at best and stupid at worst, he may develop the habit of expecting a fight just to get decent service!

What Do Customers Really Want?

Many years ago, the White House Department of Consumer Affairs Technical Assistance Research Project conducted an important study. The team members sought to determine why Customers stop doing business with a particular organization. Here's what they found out: One percent die. Obviously, there's not much you can do about that, although if you are in health care, you might want to keep an eye on that number. Three percent move away, 5 percent buy through friends, 9 percent prefer a competitor, and 16 percent don't like the business's product or service anymore. Sixty-eight percent feel that the supplier of the product or service is disinterested or indifferent.

Sixty-eight percent do not feel cared about, so they go away. Consider the tangibles in this study. If you combine "prefer the competitor" and "don't like your product/service," it only adds up to 23 percent. Virtually three times as many people who go away do not feel cared about. If that isn't an opportunity for an ounce of prevention instead of a pound of cure, we don't know what is.

When you care about your Customer, you look for ways to apply those ounces of prevention instead of letting things deteriorate until you need the pounds of cure. We've interviewed hundreds of successful service providers—people acknowledged by their employers, managers, and peers as top of the line, best of the best, the people who get the thank-you notes and grateful phone calls from delighted Customers. Time and again they tell us that rather than assuming the positive perception of their Customers, they actively seek to shape that perception themselves. On the phone, when they're taking notes, they let their Customer know that they are taking notes rather than scribbling or typing quietly as the Customer talks on. If they find themselves waiting for a computer to finish a search, they tell the Customer about it. These service stars know that nature hates a vacuum and that when Customers don't know what's going on, they make stuff up.

Exceed Expectations

Expectations play a role in your Customer's perception of your service. If your Customer receives a higher level of service from you or from other organizations offering similar services, she comes to accept it and then expect it.

Love Thy Customer

Exceeding your Customer's expectations is like pole-vaulting at the Olympics! Over time, the bar gets set at higher and higher levels. Getting across the lowered bar is simply a minimum entry requirement for later stages of the event. A satisfied Customer is a low bar that wins nothing, because if you set the bar that you're aiming for with your Customer at the level of "satisfied" and miss, even by only a little bit, you wind up with a dissatisfied Customer. You lose his confidence and quite possibly his business. Set the bar higher—at Customer delight instead of satisfaction. Now if you try to exceed your Customer's expectations, and you miss by just a bit, you still wind up with a satisfied Customer because at the least you meet his expectations. Since you may not specifically know your Customer's expectations, it makes sense that you should always set the bar high—to raise your chance of shaping a positive perception.

To weave the kind of tapestry of service that delights your Customer, you must exceed your Customer's expectations in the moments of truth in which perception is shaped. Thus, going beyond the expected is an essential service goal for you to have in mind.

As Mary entered the reception area, she was still shaking her head in amazement. A young, smartly dressed gentleman had greeted her as she pulled up to the clinic and had explained to her that since the building's parking lot was full, they had made arrangements with a local garage for overflow parking. He then offered to park her car for her and have it waiting for her at the end of her appointment.

"How much is this going to cost?" asked Mary.

"Nothing," replied the young man. "It's our pleasure to be of service."

Now Mary stood looking around the office. Something about it seemed delightfully different, but she couldn't put her finger on why. The entire place was clean and organized. The magazines were in perfect order, and there were no toys strewn about the floor. But there was something more, something truly out of the ordinary. Then it suddenly dawned on her: No one was waiting in the waiting room!

Before she could consider it further, the receptionist smiled and said, "Mary Stern, I presume?" As Mary nodded, the receptionist continued, "Welcome. Please have a seat. Your doctor will be with you shortly. Can I get you some tea?"

"Sure," said Mary.

The receptionist came out from behind her desk and walked casually to the tea service in the corner of the waiting room.

"I hadn't noticed that there, "said Mary apologetically. "I can get it myself."

"Oh no, that's fine, allow me," said the receptionist, handing Mary a beautiful ceramic mug.

The chair in which Mary was now seated, sipping her tea, felt exceptionally comfortable, as if it was molding itself to her anatomy. Yet before she had fully settled in, the receptionist said, "Okay, Mary, your doctor will see you now."

Stunned, Mary looked at her watch. It was 1:00 p.m. She looked at the clock on the wall, and it confirmed the time. She reached into her pocket and looked at her appointment card. It, too, said 1:00 p.m.! "Wow," she thought, "this place is incredible." And as she was escorted to the examining room, she began compiling a mental list of friends and associates who she would just have to tell about this place. ❧

> I honor thee when counting cost
> Of trouble gained, referral lost

- ❤ Service is more about perception than reality.

- ❤ Any moment that makes an impression is a moment of truth.

- ❤ It's the little things that make the biggest impression.

- ❤ Customers want to know you care.

- ❤ Know and then exceed thy Customer's expectations

CHAPTER 2

Welcome Thy Customer

I love thee at the center of
All thoughts and actions, choices too

Bob was tired. It seemed that everything that could go wrong on this trip had gone wrong. He should have arrived at his hotel hours ago. Now, with every tick of the clock, he watched his sleeping time trickle away. Thankfully, there was only one guest ahead of him in the check-in line. But five minutes passed, and Bob was still standing in the same spot, watching the clock with a sense of growing despair as the woman behind the counter moved in slow motion filling out paperwork, scanned a computer screen, and then disappeared into a room behind the desk. "What are they doing? I've purchased cars faster than this!" thought Bob. The woman returned, seemed to go through all the same motions again, but finally the guest in front of him gathered her keys and moved away from the counter. Bob looked down to pick up his bags, but when he looked up, the woman behind the counter was gone, and he was alone in the front of the line. Another minute ticked by. Finally, the woman returned and said to him, "Yes, what can I do for you?"

Love Thy Customer

Bob thought he could see the light at the end of the tunnel. "I'm checking in. My name is Bob Rupert."

The woman looked down at her computer and said, "Bob Robert. Hmmm. It doesn't look like I have a reservation for you." Apparently, the light was an approaching train.

"Ah, no, the name is Rupert, not Robert, Rupert with a u." Bob hated it when people botched his name.

The woman continued to look at her computer and said, "Nope, no reservation."

Bob's heart seemed to stop beating. "This can't be happening," he told himself.

"Do you have a confirmation number?" the woman asked.

Bob sighed as he felt more of his minimal sleep time ticking away. "I do have a confirmation number on my laptop," Bob replied, "but I think it's got another virus, it takes forever to boot up, and I'm exhausted. Do you really need that? Is the hotel full?"

"No," she said, "We have plenty of rooms. But I'll need that number to find your reservation."

Bob, showing a great deal of restraint, said, "Look, just give me a room. Forget the number!" But before she could reply, Bob noticed the clock on the wall behind her. It showed an hour later than his watch. "Oh no! That clock isn't right, is it?"

"Yes," she replied, still typing away on the computer. "It certainly is."

"Oh, man! I thought we were in the Pacific time zone," Bob

whined. *"This is mountain time! I can't believe it. I have to get up really early and another hour of sleep has just vanished before my eyes."*

"Uh-huh," the woman said matter-of-factly. *"Do you have that number?"*

"Can't you give me a room without it?" pleaded Bob.

"Sorry, I can't do that."

Bob had had enough. *"I want to speak to the manager, please."*

Without saying anything more, she gave Bob a look that made his blood run cold and then turned and walked into the room behind the counter.

Another minute or several went by, and finally, the manager came out. He looked at Bob and said, *"What seems to be the problem?"*

Bob said, *"She didn't tell you?"*

"No," said the manager. *"She just told me there was some guy who wants to talk to me. What's the problem?"*

Feeling completely defeated, Bob sighed and then began from the top, as yet more sleeping time slowly ticked away. 🌹

Give a Greeting Right Away

Have you tried to check in to a hotel and been left to stand and wait and watch for long minutes as the front desk person stared at his computer? Seconds become minutes, and minutes seem to stretch into hours, and in the hours that pass in those minutes, frustration builds and first impressions turn dark and uninviting. In the first moment of truth with your Customer, you have the opportunity to create a warm welcome that sets the tone for the entire relationship. Nothing matches the importance of acknowledging the presence of your Customer. And in this, as in most things in life, timing is everything. It has to happen right away. Unless your activity pertains to national security or a medical emergency, look up, smile, and make eye contact with your Customer. It doesn't take long, but the effects are lasting. Then, if you must complete what you were doing, say something considerate, like, "I'll be right with you. Thank you for your patience."

You only have one chance to make a first impression. What impression do your words create for your Customer? What perception do you want your Customer to have? Consider carefully the first words your Customer hears from you. Whether it's "Wait a minute" or "How can I help you?" you will set the tone for all that follows. In fact, at the tone, people take things personally, so make sure that your voice tone sounds like you mean what you say! Have you ever been told to "Have a nice day" by someone who didn't sound like she meant it? You set the tone of your relationship with welcoming words that actually sound welcoming!

And smile when you offer your greeting! A smile is universal, cross-cultural, and means the same thing everywhere. Even on the phone, smiling matters. There is a direct correlation between how you look and how you sound over the phone. Your posture and facial expressions are reflected automatically in the sound of your voice. And when you smile, the effect on the way you feel is immediate. It comes through your voice tone and lifts up your energy to a better place. This is why, in a growing number of call centers, people have mirrors on their desks with the word *SMILE* printed on them! Whenever companies use this simple device, their Customer satisfaction scores skyrocket!

In the first moment of truth, you can better Love Thy Customer when you stop whatever else you are doing for at least that moment, acknowledge your Customer immediately with a smile and some eye contact, and, with a pleasant tone in your voice, offer some welcoming words.

Get a Name

One simple way to make your Customer feel welcome is to use her name correctly. If you have trouble remembering names, create a visual connection in your mind. For example, if the Customer's name is Brook, you can picture a babbling brook. Or imagine that each Customer you meet for the first time is wearing a name tag. As soon as you have a name to go with that Customer, see it printed on the name tag. On the phone? Jot down the name the first moment you hear it. Repeating your Customer's name at least once during a conversation can help you to remember. Incorporate it into the next thing you say. "Hello, Brook, how can I help you?"

Paying attention is essential in the first moments of truth, particularly when it comes to titles. Someone who recently went through a bitter divorce probably won't like hearing "Mrs." even one more time. Call a teenager "Mister," and he'll think you're talking to his dad. And when someone introduces herself as a "doctor," that's usually a sign that she's spent a lot of time, money, and energy to become one, and she'd like to get a little extra mileage or leverage out of the title!

Customers who give you a formal name prefer it, and those who give you an informal name prefer that. Only switch from formal to informal when you have permission. And if you're ever unsure about how to address your Customer, ask! Spelling matters, too. Your Customers don't like doing business with companies that try to destroy their family's good name by misspelling it. Then be sure that you make note of the spelling so that future moments of truth help you build Customer delight.

Be a Great Host

You want your Customer to feel welcome, so remember the power of making small talk! If, during a phone call, you hear a cat's meow on the other end of the line and your Customer says, "Not now, Rollie," you might reply, "Oh, you have a cat.

True Love

What kind of cat is Rollie?" This communicates that you have an interest in your Customer's life. And that's powerful because most people like to talk at least a little bit about themselves. It gives them the feeling of connection.

However, not everyone likes small talk, and you don't want to digress so far that your Customer becomes irritated or an unwilling participant in your tangent! Talking about your Customer's cat is one thing, but telling her about your cat is something else entirely. When you say "I love cats! I used to have a cat, several in fact! When I was a child, my parents brought home a calico cat that was really smart and independent," you run the risk of your Customer hearing, "Blah blah blah de blah blah," and becoming frustrated and impatient. Instead, try to balance your small talk by keeping your focus on your Customer and by bringing all small talk back around to the business interest at hand.

A warm welcome includes introductions to other people in your organization. Have you ever had the experience of explaining your story or problem to a service Rep who then transferred you to someone else, who then asked you to explain your problem again, and then that person transferred you to yet another person, who asked you to explain it yet again? If you have, then it's easy to understand the power of making necessary introductions.

If your Customer needs to talk to someone in another

department, make sure the call gets transferred to the appropriate party in a welcoming way! Brief the next service Rep by providing a concise summary of all the information you've collected so far. In that way, the next Rep can give a higher quality of service by picking up where you left off instead of leaving your Customer with the feeling that he is spinning his wheels and getting nowhere. Make sure that the next Rep has your Customer's name, with the correct pronunciation, and, if possible, introduce your Customer personally to the next Rep. Then, if the next service Rep in the service chain of events also makes the Customer feel welcome by saying the Customer's name and briefly describing her understanding of the Customer's situation, your Customer will know that progress is being made, and a better time and more positive experience will be had by all.

Bob was tired. It seemed that everything that could go wrong on this trip had gone wrong. He should have arrived at his hotel hours ago. Now, with every tick of the clock, he knew his sleeping time was ticking away. Luckily, it seemed, there was only one guest ahead of him in the check-in line. As soon as he put his bags down, the woman at the front desk looked up from what she was doing, gave him a big smile, and said, "I'll be with you in just a moment. Thanks for your patience!" A few taps on the keyboard and a big smile later, she had finished checking in the guest in front of him. She smiled at him again and said, "Are you checking in?"

True Love

"Yes," Bob replied. "I'm Bob Rupert."

"Oh yes, Mr. Rupert, we've been expecting you! I'm Jennifer. Welcome. You're a bit late. Has it been a rough day?"

Bob rolled his eyes and grinned bashfully, "Yes, is sure has. You wouldn't believe it. Everything that could go wrong did go wrong. Weather delays, then a mechanical delay, and they gave away my first-class seat. I was crammed like a sardine in a middle seat between two giants."

All the while she looked him in the eyes, nodded her head, and made empathetic sounds. "Oh, that's terrible. Well, you're safe now. Let us be your home away from home. We'll get you to your room as quickly as possible so that you can get some rest."

Bob noticed the clock on the wall behind her. It showed an hour later than his watch. "Oh no! That clock isn't right, is it?"

"Yes," she replied, and the sound of concern in her voice matched the sound of concern in his. "Why?" she asked.

Bob whined, "Oh no, I thought we were in the Pacific time zone, but this is mountain time. I have to get up really early, and another hour of sleep has just vanished before my very eyes."

"Oh gosh, Mr. Rupert, that's terrible," she empathized, "Listen. Here's your key. Maybe we can save you at least a little time in the morning. Would you like to put in your breakfast order for room service now so that you don't have to think about it in the morning? I have a menu right here."

"Thank you, that's really kind. And it's a great idea," said Bob.

Love Thy Customer

As Bob filled out the breakfast card, Jennifer tapped away at the computer again and made a new key. As Bob handed the card back to her, she handed him the key and said, "I just changed your room. You're going to be in one of our newly upgraded rooms with one of the most comfy beds you've ever slept in. Maybe you can't sleep a long time, but at least you'll sleep really well in the little time you have." Bob felt the stress of the day slowly draining away. "Is there anything else I can do for you? Perhaps have your shoes polished while you sleep? Just leave them outside your door. I'll have them ready for you when your breakfast is served." Jennifer assured him. "And if there is anything else we can do to make you feel welcome, please don't hesitate to ask. I'm glad you made it. Now go get some rest." Bob was glad he made it too! With a smile on his tired face, he headed off to bed. ❧

I love thee at the center of
All thoughts and actions, choices too

❤ Give a greeting right away.

❤ Your tone is more important than your words.

❤ Smile, even when you are on the phone.

❤ Learn and use thy Customer's name (and title) correctly.

❤ Create a warm welcome with introductions and transfers.

CHAPTER 3

Heal Thy Customer

I help thee in thy painful hour
I care for thee with helping heart
With cooling words and warming smile

Hal tapped his foot more with impatience than with the beat of the music, which wasn't half bad. There was a deadline looming, and he needed to reconfigure the keyboard or else go back to the old broken one. His next move depended on the answer to one simple question, and he hoped to get that answer quickly. Since he had never called this company before for help, he didn't know what to expect. But it was a big, well-known company, so surely it must have reasonably decent help. So far, the hold time was a little excessive, but at least the company had good taste in music.

Suddenly, the music stopped. Hal heard a couple of clicks and then a quiet robotic voice said, "What is your product?" Hal thought it must be one of those automated voice systems. The voice repeated, "What is your product?" It was a little disconcerting.

Hal stammered and said, "The g-gyro wireless k-keyboard."

The monotone voice continued, "Your serial number?"

"Um, well, okay," stammered Hal.

"Sir, your serial number?" the voice asked.

Maybe it isn't a robot, thought Hal. The keyboard was on the other side of the house. Hal had moved while on hold. "I'll have to get it."

"I'll wait," came the reply.

Hmmm, thought Hal, I don't think this is an automated system. He volunteered, "It's in my office, on the other side of my house."

"I'll wait," replied the voice again.

Okay, thought Hal, this is pretty weird. I think she's a person, but she sounds like a machine! He decided to test his theory. "How's your day going?"

"Sir, I need the serial number," replied the voice.

Hah! It is a person, Hal said to himself. Now there was only silence as he raced back to his home office. "Okay, the number is a little hard to read, but it looks like CXV1847672. I'm calling with a question. . . . "

The voice cut him off with a firm, "What is the model number?"

Hal took a deep breath. What a waste of time, he thought, as he gave her the model number.

As Hal once again tried to ask his question, the voice cut him off with, "What is your serial number?"

True Love

Hal had had enough. He raised his voice, "We already did that!"

She said, "I'm sorry. I mean your phone number."

Hal gave her his number.

"And what is your name?"

Impatient now, Hal snapped, "Hal Rothman! Look, I just want to ask a question, and I'm in a hurry."

She replied, "I need to get this information." Hal took another deep breath as she asked for his address.

"That's it!" Hal shouted, "I just want to ask a question, and I am not giving you my address. I am not registering for anything right now. I bought this stupid keyboard, and I just called to ask a question about it!"

She simply said, "Fine. What is your question?"

Hal explained that he wanted to remap two keys and wanted to know if there was any software, third party or otherwise, that the company could recommend for that purpose.

"The only software we have is what comes with the product."

Hal noted that her listening skills were on par with her empathy skills. He knew that he wasn't going to get anywhere. He wasn't going to learn anything. But he had come this far, through so much, so he had to ask the final question. "I don't think you heard me. I asked if you know of any other software, third party or otherwise?"

The answer was a simple and robotic, "No."

Hal hung up the phone. He would have preferred talking to a machine. At least with a machine you don't get your hopes up.

Emotions before Solutions

Sometimes, Loving Thy Customer requires you to deal with Customer distress regarding your products and services. Sometimes your Customer's distress is so great that she needs your help before you can learn from her about the nature of her problem and the possible solutions. Emotion overrides logic when it comes to how people deal with distress. You cannot often reason with an emotional person, but you can get an emotional person to become reasonable.

One of the most common mistakes made with an upset Customer is to jump to the point of offering solutions too quickly. Your first goal should be to make sure that the Customer feels emotionally understood. Understanding does not mean that you agree or disagree. Bring up your energy level so that it more closely matches that of your Customer. Let your Customer hear that you care with the tone of your voice. Make statements of emotional empathy such as

"Oh no, that's terrible."

"I can understand why you are so upset."

"Seems like we really let you down."

"This means a lot to you."

You'll know that it's time to move on if your Customer starts to repeat the same statements over and over again. People repeat themselves when they need feedback that they've been heard and understood. And one of the best kinds of feedback you can give is *backtracking*. Backtracking is what we call it when you say back at least some of what has been said to you. The Customer's actual words are important, because words are symbols that represent a person's experience. If you change your Customer's words into your own, "In other words . . . " or "What you're really trying to say," you run the risk of your Customer correcting you, "No, actually, what I'm really trying to say is the thing I said right before that thing you said that I said that I didn't say!" To find out the meaning of words, clarify by asking questions such as who, what, where, when, and how. Backtracking indicates that you are listening, and clarification questions indicate that you care. Put them together and people feel heard and understood.

Once you've clarified the who, what, where, when, and how information of your Customer's distress, summarize it in a single statement. And before transitioning to problem solving, ask a confirmation question, such as

"Anything else?"

"Do you feel like I understand?"

If the Customer confirms that your understanding is correct, it's time to ask, "Shall we solve your problem?" or "Would you like to hear what we can do for you?" When your Customer says "Yes!" that's a signal that it's time to complete the transition from problem finding to problem solving.

Strong feelings interfere with clear thinking. Emotion often blocks logic. When people are truly upset, it's like their brain is not connected to their mouth. Therefore, their distress does the talking, and it may say some very unpleasant things. But you can help your Customer to express her distress and get it out of her system. Just take a little time to listen, and then let her know that you want to help. Better yet, you can know the most common causes of distress and prevent them.

Keep Your Promises

A broken promise causes distress. How this happens is understandable, and the method of help is a simple one. When things go wrong, as they sometimes will, admit to a mistake, and apologize for it. This may be the first step of the long journey toward making amends, or it may be the entire journey in a single step. Most people will understand if you give a heart-felt apology. Break a promise twice, though, and almost no amount of apologizing will compensate for the damage done!

When you make a commitment to your Customer, be certain that you can and will keep it. You prevent broken promises when you underpromise and overdeliver. Should you fail to deliver, you'll wind up with an angry or upset Customer who is going to have a hard time trusting you again.

We've asked service Reps why they make such promises, and the typical reply is "Because our competitors do!" or " It feels good to tell a Customer what he wants to hear." Sometimes, you'll find yourself dealing with the consequences of a broken promise made by someone else. For example, salespeople may promise the sun, moon, stars, and sky in order to gain someone's business—and then service Reps have to explain to the Customer that they don't actually provide those services. The problem with this kind of departmental disconnect is that credibility is lost, and the long-term relationship with the Customer is damaged.

We know of one company that had just this problem, and here's how that company solved it. The company made sure that every salesperson spent a week in the service department and every service Rep spent a week with the sales department. In this way, people representing both sides of the service puzzle saw how they fit together and were able to help each other to help their shared Customers. They were able to clearly define what they could absolutely, positively deliver every time, and they promised each other to promise only that! The result? By exceeding their promises with Customers, they impressed them and gained market share.

If you consistently underpromise and overdeliver in both small matters and matters of great importance, you'll gain a delighted Customer every time!

Be Polite

Rudeness causes Customer distress. And like beauty, rudeness is in the eye of the beholder. Oh yes, we know. There are incredible time pressures on you to perform your job, and sometimes this causes you to want to handle your Customer quickly and cut the visit short. While making good use of limited time is surely wise, Customers don't want to be handled. They want to be helped, and they want to feel like you have the time to help.

Trying to get rid of a Customer in the shortest amount of time is short-term thinking that's likely to cost you more time than had you taken the time to begin with. Sometimes you've got to slow down in order to hurry things up. Take the time to listen up front, and you free up time sooner rather than later. To help a Customer who feels that she's been treated rudely or, better still, to make certain that no Customer feels that way, you've got to take the time and indicate that you've got the time. If time is running short, give the Customer your time frame, and then offer her your undivided attention.

Let Them Know You're Listening

The idea that no one is listening is a cause of Customer distress. If a Customer has ever told you that you're not listening and you heard him say it, you may have wondered how he could possibly think that no one was listening. This is what happens when questions are asked that are not about the Customer's problem or when answers are offered to questions that haven't been asked.

Backtracking before answering questions eliminates this cause. When you say back some of what your Customer has said to you, using his own words instead of yours, you get to hear the question a second time so that you can make certain that you're answering the question you've been asked. When a Customer asks a question, always repeat back the question before answering it!

Have a Caring Attitude

Indifference causes Customer distress. Indifference is conveyed by a low energy level and a disinterested voice tone. The fact is, at the tone, people take things personally. Voice tone sends what is commonly referred to as an ego message that tells your Customer whether you care about her or not.

Your voice tone tends to reflect your own emotional state in any given moment. And when your tone does not match your words, your words will be ignored. If you have an uncomfortable interaction with a coworker or a previous Customer, any suppressed thoughts and feelings you have about that interaction may leak out in your interaction with the next Customer, who then proceeds to take it personally. As a service professional, you must pay close attention to the sound of your voice. If you catch your tone going in a different direction than your words, call attention to it and account for it so that your Customer doesn't take it personally.

Indifference and disinterest is also what the Customer experiences when something goes wrong and nobody addresses it. When it is clear that nothing you can say will eliminate the Customer's problem, try an apology. Then offer to investigate what happened and report back to the Customer. "Nothing I say or do will take away the fact that this happened to you, but here is what I can do for you. I can find out what went wrong, and I can do my best to make sure that we learn from your experience so that it doesn't happen to anyone else." This is a powerful statement to the Customer that speaks volumes about your caring and integrity. The Customer may even tell you that such effort is unnecessary. If the Customer takes you up on your offer, however, make sure to do what you say you will do.

Have a Can-Do Attitude

Few things can cause the distress of dealing with somebody who has a "can't-do" attitude. Consider, if you will, the meaning of the word *can't*. Basically, the word *can't* is a statement of commitment! It's like saying, "You can count on me . . . *not* to do that! Here's what I can . . . *not* do for you!"

There are all kinds of words that lead Customers to believe that they are talking to an outsider instead of an insider. Take the word *they*, for example. Who is "they"? Whenever you say *they* while referring to your organization, you are telling your Customer that you are as out of the loop as your Customer! Customers don't want to talk to outsiders. They're hoping to talk to insiders.

Then there's the famous disclaimer, "Hey, I just work here." And the Customer thinks, "No you don't!" Or how about, "Look, I don't write the policies." The Customer begins silently screaming, "Author, Author!"

And perhaps the ultimate unhelpful "can't-do" disclaimer: "You're the only person who has complained about this." First of all, so what? When you consider that only 4 of 100 unhappy

Customers complain to the offending party because the other 96 figure it won't do any good, then the 4 who speak up are giving you valuable feedback. And just about everybody will tell a lot of other people. This is called *word-of-mouth advertising,* and it can poison a whole community against you! And the worst part is, you won't know about it until it's too late.

Beware of Explanations

Perhaps the most determined form of distress-producing unhelpfulness is something we call "dextification." This is a made-up word that stands for "defense, explanation, and justification." "Dextification" conveys the idea in the Customer's thought processes that he is dealing with someone who is weak, defensive, and completely out of the loop as far as providing service.

Why would someone communicate in a way that conveys such weakness? Sadly, it's the well-intentioned effort to tell someone the truth. Now, don't get us wrong. Sometimes you have to tell your Customer the truth. But there is a time and place for it—and a time when it can backfire and actually have the reverse effect of telling the Customer that your whole system is indifferent to her needs. Generally speaking, Customers only need to know what they actually need to know. If it isn't possible to solve a problem, then you have a duty to inform your Customer so that she can make other plans. If there is a problem with your system but you can solve that problem, telling the Customer what isn't working may only serve to shake her confidence in your organization.

Of course, if the Customer asks for an explanation, it is appropriate to offer one. Yet be warned that Customers will get sick of hearing your explanation if it is long, complicated, or confusing. And if you're offering this requested explanation over the phone, it is in your interest to check in with the Customer after a minute or two and ask if she wants to hear more.

So when is it appropriate to "dextify"? When the information can relieve your Customer's fear. If you can tell the Customer not only what has gone wrong but also why he will never have to worry about the problem occurring again, then it is worth taking the time to do so—but only *after* you have solved the present problem.

Hal *tapped his foot more with impatience than with the beat of the music, which wasn't half bad. There was a deadline looming, and he needed to reconfigure the keyboard or else go back to the old broken one. His next move depended on the answer to one simple question, and he hoped to get that answer quickly. Since he had never called this company before for help, he didn't know what to expect. But it was a big, well-known company, so surely it must have reasonably decent help. So far, the hold time was* a little excessive, but at least the company had good taste in music.

Suddenly the music stopped, and a cheerful voice said, "Hi there, I'm Marie, and I'm sorry you were on hold for so long. To whom am I speaking?"

"My name is Hal."

"And what product are you calling about?" Marie asked.

Hal said, "The gyro wireless keyboard."

To which Marie said, "Do you happen to have your serial number? It's a teeny number on the bottom."

"Um, well, okay," said Hal. "While I was on hold, I went to the other side of the house."

Marie said, "I understand. No problem. Take your time."

Hal found the keyboard and said, "Okay, the number is a little hard to read, but it looks like CXV1847672."

"Yes," said Marie, "that's it! And while you're there, if you wouldn't mind, can I have the model number? It's just above the serial number."

Hal provided the model number.

Then Marie asked, "Can I get some other information from you? We like to keep track of our Customers."

Hal said, "Actually, I am in a hurry, I have a deadline. I'm already on your e-mail list, and I just have an urgent question that I'm hoping you can answer."

True Love

Marie empathized, "Uh-oh, a deadline!" And then with enthusiasm she said, "Well, what are we waiting for? Let's get to it. What is your question?"

Hal explained that he wanted to remap two keys and asked if there was any software, third party or otherwise, that Marie knew of.

Marie said, "The software we ship with the keyboard does not allow you to do that. I can't say that I know specifically of a third-party application that does what you're after. Still, it seems like the kind of thing that would exist. I'm sorry that I'm not able to provide you with a solution. However, I can direct you to a couple of Web sites where you might find such a thing, and we also have a user forum where you might be able to get some help. Can I give you those Internet addresses?"

"Absolutely! That's great," said Hal. "That's exactly what I was hoping for!" 🌹

I help thee in thy painful hour
I care for thee with helping heart
With cooling words and warming smile

❤ Be polite and soothe emotion before offering solutions.

❤ Be certain when you promise and then do better.

❤ Backtracking says you're listening; asking questions says you care.

❤ Focus on what you can do rather than on what you cannot do.

❤ Customers want to be helped, not handled.

CHAPTER 4

Educate Thy Customer

I teach thee when thy need is great
For learning all our ways
If failing that, I know t'would be
My business gone if not for thee

"**C**ome on, work!" *Sally had tried whining, pleading, begging, and now demanding, but her computer apparently couldn't care less. She scoured her brain for any more possibilities other than having to call the IT department. She still cringed when she thought of her last interaction with Ralph. "Maybe he'll be out, and I'll get that new person. What was her name?" The new IT hire didn't know as much as Ralph, but at least Sally knew that she was helpful.*

Sally dialed. The voice on the other end said, "Yeah, Ralph here."

"Um, ah, yes, ah, hi Ralph. This is Sally in Finance. . . ."

Ralph cut her off with a curt, "What did you do to your computer now?"

From someone else, that might have been funny, but Ralph's tone was anything but funny.

"Well I don't think I did anything to my computer, but when I try to save a spreadsheet, I get an error message."

Ralph sighed a long and condescending sigh. "I hope I am not interrupting anything," *said Sally, trying desperately to win favor.*

"No, I just sit around here playing video games all day," *Ralph replied sarcastically.* "What do you think?"

Sally stumbled, "I'm sorry. I didn't mean anything by it. I was just trying to be polite"—something you don't know a thing about, *she thought to herself.*

"So what is the error message?" *Ralph demanded.*

"Well, um, hang on. I'll have to get it back on my screen again."

Ralph made another unintelligible and unpleasant sound. "Are we there yet?" *he said impatiently.*

"Hang on . . ."

"No," *Ralph replied immediately.* "How about you hang on, and I hang up. I don't have time for your incompetence today. I can't believe they trust you people with computers."

"Okay, I've got the error message back," *said Sally sheepishly.*

"Look," *Ralph said,* "It's obvious you attempted to quit a running instance of the application object for that instance. By design, the application does not quit an instance of itself unless all *external references are released. Did you release all external references before quitting the application? Did you?" he demanded.*

"Huh?" said Sally, her mind drowning in a sea of emotion and confusion. ⚘

Learning Precedes Teaching

In an age of information—and information overload—it is not enough to honor your Customer, or to welcome her, or even to comfort and help her heal. Sometimes, your Customer must depend on you to teach her what she needs to know in order to make the best use of your products and services. You provide the essential educational link.

There are two dimensions to education. The first is learning, and the second is teaching. Quite often learning *precedes* teaching. Together, these two dimensions feed each other because every Customer presents you with an opportunity to learn more about your Customer's needs, which makes you better able to educate your Customer, which leads to more business and more opportunities to learn!

There are two important times to learn before trying to teach anything to a Customer. First, when a Customer asks a question that you can't answer! Rather than giving an answer that is weak at best and makes you look bad at worst, say, "You deserve a high-quality answer to your question. Let me get back to you." And you set up a time to share this information after you've had a chance to do a little research.

The other instance when learning precedes teaching is when something goes wrong! In the higher education of Loving Thy Customer, this is a learning moment because one always can learn from experience. Like Sigfield Von Krunkhausen says: "Life is a hard teacher. She gives the test first and the lesson after!"

Give Learnable Lessons

First, determine if your Customer is ready to learn. Some Customers actually enjoy the opportunity for a little education, whereas others have places to go, things to do, and people to meet. Ask, "Would you like some information on how to prevent this situation in the future?"

Then use your best judgment to identify your Customer's knowledge level so that you can provide your information at a level the Customer can understand. If you oversimplify, you're wasting your Customer's time. Overcomplicate, and it may go right over your Customer's head. In either case, you could be the last to know as your Customer avoids the embarrassment of "not understanding."

In general, it is better not to give answers or instructions that are too complex over the phone. Instead, provide detailed instructions in writing, in person, by fax, or by e-mail. This avoids misunderstanding and makes good use of your Customer's time, as well as your own. It also spares your Customer the chore of taking notes and prevents him from writing down a misunderstood direction that could only compound the problem. And perhaps most important, it shows your Customer that you care enough to go the extra mile on his behalf.

"**C**ome on, work!" Sally had tried whining, pleading, begging, and now demanding, but her computer apparently couldn't care less. There was no choice but to call the IT department. She hoped that someone from the department would be available because the vice president of finance needed this spreadsheet by the end of the day.

Sally dialed. The voice on the other end said, "Yes, Lew here."

"Um, ah, yes, ah. Hi Lew, this is Sally in finance. . . . "

With a smile in his voice, Lew said, "Is your computer being a bad boy today?"

Sally laughed, "Yes, I was going to send him to the principal's office, but I thought I would call you instead."

Lew responded with, "Well, Sally, I guess you'd better tell me what horrible thing it is doing or not doing that led to me having the pleasure of your call."

Sally smiled to herself. She knew Lew must be busy. Heck,

everyone was busy these days, often working at hyperspeed, since the big merger. And although Lew had the primary responsibility for integrating the two systems, somehow he sounded like he had all the time in the world, and Sally was his only Customer. "Well I don't think I did anything differently, but when I try to save a spreadsheet, I get an error message."

"So let me make sure I understand. You have the spreadsheet open, and when you go to the file menu to save it, you get an error message?" *Lew inquired.*

"Yes," *said Sally, amazed at how quickly he had understood.*

"And is this a new spreadsheet or an old file that you are updating?"

"Well, it's old and new," *replied Sally.* "I started with an old file but then modified it and renamed it. I hope I didn't screw it up."

"No, don't worry. You didn't do anything wrong," *offered Lew reassuringly.* "Your operating system has a built-in productivity detector. If you're getting too much done, it interferes to slow you down. This kind of thing happens all the time. How much time do you have?" *asked Lew.*

"I am kind of under the gun, Lew," *said Sally,* "because the vice president of finance needs this file by the end of the day."

"I know what you mean by under gun," *smiled Lew.* "Lately it's felt like we have our backs to the wall over here in the ole' IT department. If not for the huge load of integration activities that we've earned through the merger, I would be happy to come by*

True Love

your cubicle and take care of this for you. I won't be able to do that for a couple of hours. And I know that's not going to do you any good. However, if you have 10 minutes, I can walk you through a procedure right now that not only should fix this problem, but I can also show you how to prevent things like this in the future. Interested?"

"That would be wonderful!" smiled Sally. Maybe the technology wasn't the user-friendly type, but Lew sure was! And that made all the difference in the world. 🌹

> I teach thee when thy need is great
> For learning all our ways
> If failing that, I know t'would be
> My business gone if not for thee

💜 Learn what thy Customer needs to know before offering a lesson.

💜 Offer learnable lessons that will make sense to thy Customer.

💜 Be willing to say "I don't know," and then find out.

💜 Make sure your Customer has time to learn.

💜 Consider the ideal form for the lesson (face to face, phone, e-mail).

47

CHAPTER 5

Solve Thy Customer's Problems

To do no harm, and harm undo
I help thee to relieve thy stress

Phil called his local Internet service provider (ISP) and described his video-chat problem as best he could. The ISP person interrupted him. "It could be the connection, the cable, the modem, or the computer. You're really going to have to figure out this problem yourself."

"Okay," Phil started to explain what he had already done, but the Rep cut him off again.

"Well, the first thing you should do is rule out your connection. You can do that by downloading a file from the fiber network's Web site."

"Okay," replied Phil, doing his best to be polite and cooperative. "So where do I get that file?"

"From the fiber network. Call them and ask for it." He gave Phil the phone number.

"What do I do with this file once they tell me how to find it?" asked Phil.

"You measure the time it takes to download."

"Oh," said Phil. "Then what?"

"Call me back."

Darn, thought Phil, but so be it. He thanked the Rep, hung up, and then dialed the fiber network. He got through to a person right away. That's a good sign, thought Phil. But the fiber network Rep cut him off as he was explaining that he needed the address for a file on their Web site.

"I don't know anything about that. Call your ISP," was the Rep's advice.

Phil said, "Well, I don't know anything about it either. But I did call my ISP, and I was told to call you, the fiber network, and I was told that you would know what that file was and where I could find it."

She simply said, "I don't." Her cold apathy gave Phil a shiver down his spine.

Nevertheless, still hoping for some assistance, he inquired, "Do you think you could ask somebody else?"

"No!" she replied firmly. "I said you have to call your ISP and work it out through them."

Phil sighed, hung up, and called his ISP again. He talked to the same person, a guy named Paul, and explained what had just happened.

Paul said, "Sorry you had to deal with that. Let me do some research, and I'll get back to you in 15 minutes."

A half hour later, Phil still hadn't heard anything, so he called again. Paul said, "Oh, I gave it to Dave, and he should have got-ten back to you. Hang on a second." Several minutes passed, then Paul came back and said, "Dave is out today. No wonder he hasn't e-mailed you." ⚘

Own the Problem

If you are called on to solve a problem, start by taking charge over it rather than passing it back or shifting it elsewhere. The basic idea is that if the problem comes to you, its solution must happen through you, so you "own" that problem until either it is resolved or someone else takes ownership of it.

All your Customers have unique problems and challenges, they make unusual requests, they see things in strange and wonderfully confusing ways, and they seek solutions to prob-lems you've never even imagined—let alone solved. They often will demand that you take them to destinations where no one has gone before, and they may or may not give hints and clues as to where they really want to go or why they expect you to take them there. *But . . .* you still must figure out the why, the what, the who, the where, the when, and the how of it all. Detective work requires careful attention to specific details.

So be patient, persistent, and—above all—curious. Questions are your most powerful tool. Careful listening and gentle probing are your means to helping your Customer divulge the clues you'll need to solve even the most convoluted and unusual human request.

Keep Records, Provide Reports

Since the information you work with will form the foundation of the paper or electronic trail that describes your Customer's relationship with you and your organization, future generations may well depend on your accuracy. Therefore, shorthand is not enough, and your accuracy is essential. Keep great records because chances are you're going to need them or someone else will. Good record keeping will help you to track recurring problems and get to the root cause. Remember to keep track of who was involved, what specifically happened, where and when it happened, and how it happened! And when possible, include the cost of the problem and dealing with it (your time and company resources, as well as any suggestions about preventing the problem in the future).

When a problem takes more than a visit or a call to resolve, you can use your records to create reports that keep your Customer informed about progress. Customers don't like to be left hanging, wondering about what's happening with their service requests. You can prevent additional problems and delight your Customer by providing timely information on what you're doing on her behalf. Include, when possible, an outline of your plan and an expected timetable so that your Customer isn't left to guess about what is going on. Keep a copy of all reports as part of your ongoing records in case other service Reps get involved in the case. In this way, everyone can know what's going on by checking the records until a particular case is closed.

Dig a Little Deeper

Sometimes the problem is not what the Customer thinks it is. The only way to be sure is to dig a little deeper to find the real problem. Whenever you find that you cannot do what you're being asked to do, go deeper to find other and better ways to Serve Thy Customer.

A tech support Rep received a frantic call from a customer. The customer had to produce a company newsletter in three days. Based on her responses to the Rep's initial questions, it seemed that her knowledge of the program was minimal. Further inquiries revealed that the Customer had never used the program before. The Rep politely explained that it was unlikely she would be able to complete her project in three days given the complexity of the program and the magnitude of the project. This information triggered a temper tantrum. The Rep was able to calm the Customer down and dig deeper for more details. "Obviously, this is a very important project to you, and I understand that it is essential that it be done by Friday," said the Rep. "Can I ask you why it must be done by Friday?" The Customer explained that she was new at the company, and although she had not been hired for her abilities in desktop publishing, her boss had dropped the manual for the program on her desk and "suggested" that she get a company newsletter done by Friday. Thus the real problem was not the newsletter; it was the fact that she was about to fail in the eyes of her boss on her first project. The Rep suggested that she connect him with her boss. He then explained to her boss that the desktop publishing software program was too complex to master in just a few days. The boss said he hadn't realized that and told his new employee to take all the time she needed to master the program.

Ask How You're Doing

You can use questions to get feedback from your Customer about how your service is perceived and received. Our favorite feedback tool is something we call *Sherlock's Simple Questions*. First, tell your Customer why you want to get some feedback. "I want to provide you with the best service that I can, and I need your help to accomplish this. May I ask you a few questions so that I can apply your feedback to my efforts on your behalf?" Then ask, "What am I already doing for you that I could be doing better?" Ask, "What am I not doing that I should be doing?" Ask, "What am I doing that I should stop doing because you don't find it valuable or helpful?" Follow up each of these questions with the evidence question: "How would you know?" When people tell you what they're looking for, listening for, hoping for, and waiting for, that information allows you to add their perception of you to your service efforts. In this way, you can reduce the difficulty of your work and raise the quality of your service dramatically.

Phil called his local ISP and explained his problem. After listening, a service Rep named Paul said, "Excuse me for interrupting, I just want to make sure that I've understood you correctly. Would you mind if I tell you what I've heard so far?"

Phil was pleased and said, "Sure, go ahead!"

Paul summarized the information he'd written down, and by the time he'd reviewed what he'd written, he knew what questions he still needed to ask. "Did you try swapping out the cable?"

Phil replied in the affirmative.

"Did you try removing any routers on the system?"

Again, Phil said, "Yes. And," Phil continued, "I tried plugging in a different computer and had the same problem."

"Okay, then," said Paul, with a little excitement in his voice. "That only leaves two possibilities as far as I can tell. Either the connection to your home office is bad, or your modem is not work-

ing correctly. I think the modem is the most likely culprit. But the only way we can test that is if you come down to our office and pick up our loaner modem. Would that be all right with you?"

Phil was more than happy to try anything to resolve this, and he thought Paul had a good plan. "Sounds good," said Phil.

Phil headed down to his ISP's office to pick up the loaner modem. When Paul opened the door, he handed Phil the modem, along with a troubleshooting flowchart he'd put together in case Phil ever ran into connection problems in the future.

"Thanks, Paul," said Phil. "You guys are the best!"

As Phil walked back down the sidewalk toward his car, Paul smiled and said to himself, "If we're the best, it's because we love our Customers!"

To do no harm, and harm undo
I help thee to relieve thy stress

- ❤ Own thy Customer's problem (take charge).

- ❤ Keep accurate and complete records.

- ❤ Keep thy Customer informed of progress and results.

- ❤ Dig deeper for the real problem or need.

- ❤ Ask thy Customer for feedback.

CHAPTER 6

Represent Thy Customer

In reaching for my true success
I honor thee and speak for thee
Lest my business fall to worthlessness

Linda was showing Kim Lee, the new hire, "the ropes." Kim Lee first monitored Linda's calls for an hour, and then they reversed roles. Kim Lee thought that Linda had great presence on the phone, and her advice was clear and practical. Kim Lee was glad to move to this company. The company had a good reputation, and although she was happy and successful in her last job, working for this company would be a step up. Things were going smoothly until she got an irate call.

"Your receipt said that no sale is ever final," began the Customer.

"That's right, sir," Kim Lee replied cheerfully yet concerned.

"My daughter bought a pair of your jeans, brought them home, put them in the wash, and they fell apart."

"Oh no, that's terrible," empathized Kim Lee.

"We returned them to the store for an exchange, and the manager insulted my daughter and accused her of intentionally wrecking the jeans."

"I am so sorry for that, sir." Kim Lee said. "Can I arrange a refund for you?"

"No, I got the refund. I'm calling because you have a real problem with your system. That manager spent an extraordinary amount of time doing paperwork before she gave me the money. Looking at lists, writing things down, stamping and signing relentlessly. Eventually, it dawned on me why she was so rude. She didn't want to deal with your system for resolving Customer complaints. It actually made more sense to her to insult the Customers than to deal with the process of giving a refund."

"I'm sure that was very frustrating for you, sir," offered Kim Lee.

Finally, the call wrapped up. The Customer appreciated Kim Lee for listening, and Kim Lee promised to let the right people know. Linda complimented Kim Lee: "You empathized really nicely with that Customer and never took his emotions personally. Good for you. We get a lot of calls about those jeans and problems with refunds. It's part of the job."

Kim Lee inquired, "So what do we do about it? Do we have a form to fill out or a meeting where we bring it up? What is the *feedback system to let management know of these problems?"*

Linda was incredulous. "Feedback system?" And then she smiled at Kim Lee and spoke to her like she was speaking to an innocent child. "No system, Kim. But it is time to take another call. Got to keep your calls-taken numbers up and your call time down. Ready? You're back on line."

Speak for Your Customer

While "Service Representative" or some variation thereof is the way your job is titled, "Customer Representative" must be inherent to that title. Just as you are the company's voice to the Customer, you are also the Customer's voice to the company! And as your Customer's representative, you can best serve your company and your Customer by representing your Customer's needs and interests to appropriate persons and facilitating changes in rules and procedures that are not to your Customer's or organization's benefit.

There you are, on the front line, seeing up close and personal what is really going on. There is no one in your organization better suited to the task. It is absolutely crucial to your future success and to your organization's success that you serve as a feedback mechanism that advocates for change. Whether for a particular Customer with a particular problem or for all your Customers who have similar problems, you must speak up to the right people and let them know what's going on.

There are three keys to being an effective advocate, and they are based on a few simple insights into the thought processes of management. First, express yourself in writing, translate the problem or your proposed solution into language that your organization will understand, and back it up with numbers.

Put It in Writing

With a little insight into the thought process of upper management, it becomes obvious that documents speak louder than words. Use a document to create a written record, and you have a powerful point of reference that allows you to capture, develop, and share an idea about how to improve service. When you express your ideas in writing, you're more likely to think your position through logically. And a document allows a number of people to consider your information at the same time. Without a document, your words to management may go in one ear and out the other. With a document, you can better present yourself as a teammate in problem solving, and you create a tangible piece of evidence that helps you to make the case for change.

Translate the Problem

Management frequently feels overwhelmed by the pace of change and the uncertainties of the workplace. Managers also can feel caught and helpless in the very same bureaucracy that is creating the problem for your Customer. Shape your document and your message in such a way that management can receive and understand it.

Begin your document by matching your advocacy for change with your organization's mission statement, marketing slogans, or the value system that management promotes. "I know this organization cares about service. After all, we've been asked by the organization to (1) read a book, (2) attend a seminar, (3) seek out training, and so on." The person reading your ideas ought to be nodding in agreement as he looks at your document. When management says, "We've got to find ways to cut costs!" and your document states, "Here is an idea to improve our Customer service while saving us $100,000 a year," you are speaking to management's interest and therefore are more likely to pique management's interest.

Then point out your reasons for presenting your information to the particular person you are addressing. Is she the only person who can do something about the problem? Is it because you are uncertain who else to talk to? Or is it because you are going to talk to someone else, and you want this person to back you up? Make it clear why you've chosen this particular person to receive your information and ideas.

Count the Cost

Specific numbers are more compelling than broad ideas! You've got to count the cost of making a change and compare it with the cost of failing to change. This information already may be recorded in your database. But even if you don't have access to some of the numbers involved in a particular problem or don't yet know the cost of your solution, that does not constitute an obstacle. Here, in the age of information, almost all the numbers you need are all around you and easily accessed from magazines, books, and the Internet. You can draw on the numbers from similar companies or similar problems in other industries. When your advocacy is based on specific figures, whether its time wasted or money wasted, time spent or money spent, you make it worthwhile for management to spend the time to at least consider your ideas.

Then make your case. Spell everything out—as clearly and logically as you can. Distribute your document simultaneously to all the decision makers who may be involved. Follow up a few days later to see if they have any questions or considerations. Never take a consideration as a "No" but rather as just a small point to which you will need ultimately to find a solution.

True Love

Finally the call wrapped up. The Customer appreciated Kim Lee for listening, and Kim Lee promised to let the right people know. Linda complimented Kim Lee. "You empathized really nicely with that Customer and never took his emotions personally. Good for you."

"Thank you," smiled Kim Lee.

Linda continued, "That is the second one of those calls I've heard this week. So that means we need to fill out the 'Bright Idea' internal feedback form. It's really simple and only takes a minute. Here, I'll show you. When you're done, you submit it. Then be ready to talk about it at the weekly staff meeting. Sometimes management will get in touch with you ahead of time with questions. Other times they ask questions at the meeting. Maybe a project team will be assigned to eliminate any Customer-unfriendly rules or procedures. The basic guideline on this sort of thing is that if you hear a problem twice, management prefers you to fill out the form. Three times, and it is mandatory. But you don't have to wait for that. If you think of an idea or see something that needs to change externally or internally, you can use the 'Bright Idea' system. That's how we fulfill our goal of getting better all the time! And we have a fun internal competition, the winner being the one with the most bright ideas. So fill this out because there are some really cool prizes."

Kim Lee smiled and knew that she had made the right career move. ❧

Love Thy Customer

In reaching for my true success
I honor thee and speak for thee
Lest my business fall to worthlessness

- ❤ Speak up for thy Customer in your organization.

- ❤ Documents speak louder than words, so put your ideas in writing.

- ❤ Translate advocacy to match organizational mission, values, and interests.

- ❤ Present your ideas and documents to the right people.

- ❤ Specific numbers make broad ideas more compelling.

CHAPTER 7

Love Thyself

How do I love me? Let me count the ways.
I love thee every time we meet
And dream of better days

The second latté was just kicking in as Mike returned to the service desk. He probably shouldn't have gone to that concert last night, but, hey, it's not every day you get a backstage pass. On his way to work, he armed himself for the daily ordeal with candy bars and caffeine. When he began to fade a couple of hours later, he hit the espresso bar in the lobby for a quick fix. He'd be back at least once or twice today.

He wasn't sure if it was an astrological phenomenon or if every customer today just happened to be exceptionally stupid. Sure, working the service desk of a computer store wasn't the easiest of jobs considering that most the people he had to interact with each day were already ticked off about spending money to fix things that shouldn't have gone wrong in the first place. But *what did they expect? It wasn't like it was news that most computers ran buggy and virus-prone software and were made with cheap parts and that most users lacked the training to actually use them. He'd bet that half these morons still had the 12:00 blinking on their VCRs.*

His first Customer was such a loser that it took all the restraint his frazzled nervous system could muster just to keep from snatching the computer away and informing her, "I'm taking this away from you because you're too stupid to use a computer in the first place." But that would cost him his job for sure. Instead, he just simmered and stewed as he listened to her go on and on about how important it was that she get back the data on her drive because it wasn't backed up, and she had deadlines, and blah de blah, blah, blah.

"If she would just shut up for a minute," he thought, "maybe I could get on with fixing it." But he had to be polite, so he told her, "Hang on, let me check and see what our backlog is." Then he turned and walked to the back, leaving the Customer in midsentence.

When he came back two minutes later, four more people had formed a line behind her. "Probably by next Friday," he stated as a matter of fact.

"Friday!" she exclaimed. "I just told you my report was due on Thursday. I asked you if the tech could at least get it off

the drive." Her voice volume rose with the sound of panic in her voice.

Mike simmered a minute and then barked at her, "Hey, lady, don't do this to me!" And that's when the grumbling in the line behind her began in earnest. ✿

Take Care of Yourself

No job is an easy job. Wouldn't it be wonderful, though, if we could promise you nothing but great moments with Customers as a result of your tremendous efforts to give your best possible service? But we can't, because if we did, we would be over-promising and underdelivering, and you would be poorly served. Instead, here's what we *can* promise you. No matter how devoted you are, no matter how focused you are on doing the right things for the right reasons at the right time, sooner or later something will happen that will be difficult for you to deal with. It cannot be avoided because on Earth, adversity and challenge are all part of the package. However, if you invest time daily in giving yourself encouragement and support, building your energy reserves and cultivating a positive attitude, and making wise choices that contribute to a higher quality of life for you and your loved ones, you will be better prepared for dealing with difficulty, disappointment, and disaster.

Give Yourself a Break

All work and no breaks is a path to burnout. The basic rule is that for every energy loss you suffer during the day, you must replenish your energy supply. And there is a science to taking breaks, because different kinds of activities require different kinds of breaks! The general rule is to do the opposite of what you have been doing.

For example, if you have been sitting still, hunched over, or glued to the phone, then at break time, stand and stretch, walk down the hall or up a flight of stairs, and get your circulation going again. You might even grab a jump rope and step outside for a few minutes of invigorating exercise.

Of course, if you've been doing close work like staring at figures or reading documents, an effective break is to stop and look out the window, if you've got one, or at a lovely photograph or painting of a natural setting. Or close your eyes and imagine being in your favorite place of beauty, and do a quick systems check of your five senses to see how much of that place you can bring into the moment.

If your work requires lots of concentration and accuracy, switch to something playful or mindless. Use your breaks wisely to refill your energy cup, because if your cup is empty, there's nothing in it for you to give in service to others.

Give Yourself Do-Overs

With every Customer interaction, you have an invaluable opportunity to learn something new, something useful, or something empowering that can be available to you in the future. Your difficult Customers help you to learn what works and what doesn't work. Instead of letting them drain you of your motivation to live, therefore, let them inspire you to serve well, to serve better, and to give your best. After each day is done, don't relive bad Customer experiences. Give yourself a mental do-over. Replay those experiences in your mind until you handle them successfully, and then do that over and over a few more times in the privacy of your mind. This kind of replay becomes the rehearsal for your next real-world encounter.

If you have trouble with the do-over, think of someone else who would have no difficulty dealing with your problem. Imagine being that person and imagine dealing with your challenge. Find out what your model would do and then imagine that it's you doing the same thing. Mary felt that she needed to be more assertive with her Customers while still remaining professional. When she asked herself who would be a model of that ability, she thought of Katherine Hepburn. Frank wanted to be "excited by a challenge and willing to do whatever it takes." When he asked himself who would be a model for that ability, he thought of Indiana Jones. Have your role model show you what to do in the do-over and then step in and do it yourself. In this way, do-overs make Loving Thy Customer an adventure! Replay the lessons of the past in a new way, and you will be amazed at the flexibility and resourcefulness you develop as a result.

Build a Support System

With all the emphasis in this chapter on the need to love thy-self, you might come to the conclusion that it's a dog-eat-dog world and you've got to look out for number one. But the nature of service is to make a difference in the lives of others. And sometimes the greatest difference you can make is to allow others to make a difference in your life! To truly go beyond the expectations of your Customer while bringing out the best in yourself, you've got to remember to let others help you!

You are not alone. You need friends who will listen to you and understand your difficulties. You need colleagues with whom to share information about what's working and what isn't working. And you need creative partners who can brain-storm and co-create with you.

Your supervisor is a part of your support system too, because your supervisor can provide you with valuable feed-back about how you're doing and what needs to be done. You

may want to find a mentor, someone to offer you encouragement and suggestions, and teachers who can help you acquire
knowledge and training. Above all, you need role models for
inspiration and motivation.

Support doesn't usually just appear in our lives. You must
identify the kinds of support you want and the kinds of support
you need and then reach out to the world around you to build
a safety net that is diverse enough to support you in the best
of times and the worst of times.

Keep Your Perspective

Whenever your job becomes overwhelming and you feel like
throwing in the towel, just remember that you got your depth
perception when you were a little kid who kept falling down.
Difficulty strengthens you, and the "hard knocks" move you to
action because they are nature's way of saying *wake up!*

Learn from your mistakes, and they become valuable.
Overcome challenges, and you grow strong. Put things in perspective, and they won't overwhelm you. These lessons in perspective have been true in your life all along! After all, it was
the stupid things you did in life that taught you everything you
needed to get you this far. Losses teach us to appreciate what
we have. The doors of opportunity are marked "Push" and
"Pull," which is why difficult times open doors to new oppor-

tunities. In good times and in bad, it's an important part of
your job to Love Thyself.

Mike was tired from staying out late at the concert, but he was
laying off the caffeine and sugar these days. Ever since he decided to
take better care of himself, work had gotten easier and was a lot more
fun than it used to be. Now he got to work about a half hour before
the doors opened and used the time to organize his day, see what was
on the log book, and straighten up his work area. Then he made
some green tea, read a technical newsletter, and stretched. "Can't
wait for today's challenges! Bring it on!" he thought to himself. Mike
had learned to enjoy the process of getting to know his Customers,
learning about their problems, and then helping them learn to prevent them. He found the nuances of each day to be the best part of
the job, and he loved it when something out of the ordinary occurred.

He wasn't sure if it was an astrological phenomenon or the
changes in his lifestyle, but it seemed that his Customers were a
lot smarter than he used to give them credit for. Sure, working
the service desk of a computer store wasn't the easiest of jobs considering that most of the people he had to interact with each day
were already ticked off about spending money to fix things that
shouldn't have gone wrong in the first place. Who could blame
them? But they bought cheap, thinking it would save them
money, and he understood; he'd done it himself. With a little
understanding and a lot of patience, he found that their chal-

lenges made his day interesting, and he enjoyed that feeling that comes from being of service.

The moment the store had opened its doors, a line began to form at his counter. "Good morning, everybody! I'll give each of you my full attention when it's your turn. Okay, let's start with you, ma'am. What's your problem, and how can I help?"

She smiled. Somehow just knowing this young man was going to help her made the problem seem like it wasn't so bad. ❧

> How do I love me? Let me count the ways.
> I love thee every time we meet
> And dream of better days

- ❤ Invest time in your energy, attitude, and construction of your support system.

- ❤ Give yourself a break, change the pace, and keep your energy live.

- ❤ Give yourself do-overs and replay unsuccessful events in new ways.

- ❤ Choose and emulate your role models based upon how you want to feel and act.

- ❤ Keep things in perspective and find opportunity in your challenges.

PART TWO

TOUGH LOVE

Empower Thyself

When time is waste, your clouded face
I love thee more for loving's sake

Understand Difficult Customers

When bad behavior is directed at you, we know it's easy to take it personally. Whether you fight with your Customer or withdraw from your Customer, you run the risk of damaging the relationship or setting in motion a chain reaction that has no end. Sooner or later, though, you're bound to discover that rule number one for dealing with Tough Customers is a simple one: "Service is personal. Difficult behavior is not." Bad behavior has more to do with the person exhibiting it than it does with you. When you're being attacked, your first priority must be to stabilize yourself. If you're off balance, the likelihood of your falling over is increased. It's not personal. It's not about you. Breathe. Let it go. Stabilize yourself.

One way to stabilize yourself is to understand why some Customers get so emotional, controlling, negative, and withdrawn. You see, no matter how much you Love Thy Customer, you will find yourself occasionally dealing with a difficult one. When it comes to difficult people, there's much to learn and much you can do, and we covered this subject in great detail in our book, *Dealing with People You Can't Stand, How to Bring Out the Best in People at Their Worst,* published by McGraw-Hill.

We think that it will be helpful to you if we cover some of that material here in the form of an overview of the subject with some helpful tips and tactics to help you when times get tough and Customers get tougher. In particular, we developed a model that we call the *Lens of Understanding.* In it, we define a normal zone where there are four basic positive intentions that drive behavior. When these intentions are thwarted, people have a stress (fight/flight) reaction that leads to increasingly difficult behavior. At any one time, any one of these intentions can become more important than the others. In fact, stress tends to polarize people into allowing one of these intentions to supersede all others. The four positive intentions are

Get It Done
Get Along
Get It Right
Get Appreciation

Have you ever dealt with a Customer who is direct and to the point, who moves the interaction with you forward as fast as possible? This behavior tells you that your Customer wants to Get It Done. Ever dealt with a customer who was chatty, who seemed more interested in you than he was in himself, who shared details of his personal life even though such details had nothing to do with his problem? This behavior tells you that your Customer wants to Get Along. Are you familiar with the Customer who is slow and methodical when it comes to the details of your service or product or her problem with either or both? This behavior tells you that your Customer wants to Get It Right. Ever had a Customer tell you about how long he's been a Customer, how valuable his business is to your organization, and how many referrals he's made? Such behavior indicates his intention to Get Appreciation from you. Depending on the primary intent driving your Customer's interaction with you, behavior changes accordingly.

Send Signals of Similarity

Reducing conflict with difficult Customers requires that you use the essential communication skill that we call *blending*. Blending is what happens when you reduce the differences between you and your Customer or send signals of similarity that let your Customer know that you're on her side. You have the power to make things better or worse, easier or harder for you to deal with, and it all depends on whether you remember to blend.

Blend with the Get It Done Customer by getting to the point and moving the interaction forward as fast as you can. Blend with the Get Along Customer by chatting in a friendly manner and putting a little time into building the relationship with him. Blend with the Get It Right Customer by staying focused on the details of the task at hand. Blend with the Get Appreciation Customer by thanking her for her business, her loyalty, and her referrals, and by acknowledging how terrible it must have been for her to drive around for an hour looking for a place to park. Blending builds rapport—that state of trust and cooperation that successful relationships depend on—and blending puts you in a position to take the lead in how the interaction turns out.

There are many ways to blend, including posture, energy level, and statements of emotional empathy. When you are face to face, you can adopt a similar body posture. When a Customer has high energy, you can up your energy level to be more like his. When you backtrack what a Customer says to you, your blending in this way lets her know that you have listened to her. When you say, "Oh, that's terrible," or "You must be so upset," or "We really let you down," you are blending. Blending builds rapport, and rapport allows you to take the lead.

However, fail to blend with these behaviors, and your Customer's behavior may change for the worse.

The good news is that you can blend with and then lead a tough Customer out of a stress response and into a positive interaction with you. This is so because communication is like a phone number. You need all the digits of a phone number, and you need to dial them in the right order. Leaving one digit out is only a 10 percent error, but your call will not get through. Dial the area code as an afterthought, and the call does not get through. In the next few chapters we will examine the "phone numbers" strategies that can help you to love even your Tough Customers.

> When time is waste, your clouded face
> I love thee more for loving's sake

- ♥ Understand and recognize positive intent in difficult behaviors.

- ♥ Get It Done, Get It Right, Get Along, and Get Appreciation.

- ♥ Send signals of similarity by blending.

CHAPTER 8

Pushy and Demanding

Of rough commands, and heated wrath
Reaction shunned and traction gained
I spring to action strong and fast
Divide the present from the past

The Customer was in his face, jabbing his finger at him and hurling accusations as fast as he could talk. "You people are idiots. You must be genetic mistakes! This is the fourth time I've been in here with the same *&#$@ problem! Either you fix it right now, or I'm going to shove it up your @#$!!!"

Joe, the service manager on duty, looked him in the eye and thought, "I don't need this garbage after what I have been through today!" He felt the heat rising under his collar. "I don't get paid enough for this kind of abuse! I could kick this guy all over this garage!"

The Customer continued yelling: "Do you guys actually fix cars here or just sell them?"

Joe tried to compose himself, but his tone dripped with disgust, "Hey, pal, calm down, and let me ask you some questions." But that's as far as he got before the Customer raised his voice another 10 decibels.

"Questions?" he screamed! "You have a work order! You have written down the problem three times already. Where's the owner of this two-bit miserable outfit? I want to speak to the owner, or I'm going to call my lawyer!"

Joe's mind reached into the future to see how his life would turn out if he just hit this Customer with a wrench. It didn't look good. Instead, he took a deep breath and looked away, trying to shake off his angry reaction. Unfortunately, the Customer reacted by raising his voice 10 more decibels. 🌹

The Tank Attack

Do you know what it feels like to be in a hurry and have the person you're talking to slow you down when taking time is something that you can barely afford?

There are actually a few reasons why people become pushy. Sometimes people are in a hurry because they've been left on hold for too long, or they've gotten the run-around before they got to you. The Tank Customer is in a Get It Done mode. Anything that takes too long or seems like a waste of time will escalate the attack. Anything perceived as forward progress will de-escalate the attack. Your goal, therefore, is to make something happen fast.

Don't waste time! When your Customer talks to you in a blunt, direct manner, be brief and professional in response. Only give details when necessary or when your Customer asks for them.

If your Customer needs to vent, let him. It's good for people to get things out of their system. But don't let your Customer vent for too long. The Tank Customer wants action, not sympathy, and not an explanation.

Backtrack the main points so that your Customer knows that you understand the problem.

Establish that you are on your Customer's side. Even when you're being treated like an enemy, there is value in saying, "I'm here to help you, and we're going to do something about this." Say it with conviction and a real take-charge attitude. Such an attitude, on its own, may calm a Tank Customer who thinks the situation is out of control.

Clarify by asking a few questions, but only after describing your own positive intent. "In order to solve your problem fast, I need to ask you some questions. This will only take a minute or two."

Focus on solutions. There is no need to explain every little detail. Give the Customer the gist of it. If he needs more information, you can be sure he'll have no trouble asking for it!

Then tell him exactly what you're going to do to deal with his problem. Stick to the facts and don't make promises you can't keep. If you have to put a Tank Customer on hold on the phone or he has to wait in a face-to-face situation, make sure to tell him why it is to his benefit and how long it will take. If logistics permit, give your Customer the option of coming back later or offer to call him back. Always be sure that he has time before trying to educate him on how best to use your system.

Joe felt something coming at him. He looked up from the service desk to see a red-faced Customer bearing down on him. This guy looked intense, so Joe took a deep breath and steadied and readied himself. The Customer was now directly across the desk. He pointed his finger at Joe and said loudly, "Are you the $^#%&@ service manager?"

"Yes, I am the service manager," said Joe. "What can I . . . "

The Customer yelled, "I can't believe this dealership! How do you stay in business? You people are idiots. You must be genetic mistakes! This is the fourth time I've been in here with the same $#%@^ problem!"

Joe raised his volume slightly but kept his tone professional, "Sir, Sir, Sir, this is the fourth time you've been here?"

The Customer continued at the same volume and intensity, "You got that right! Look, I want this car fixed right, or I'm going to shove it up your @#$!!!"

Tough Love

Joe maintained eye contact, raised his voice volume a little, and said, "That isn't right! You shouldn't have to deal with that kind of inconvenience! Four times?"

The Customer stopped for moment, looked at Joe incredulously, and then lowered his voice a bit and continued, "Yes four times! I've had to take time from work. I probably could have fixed it faster if I'd done it myself!"

With the sound of authority in his voice, Joe proclaimed, "Sir, I am here to help you. We're going to do something about this. The buck stops here." The Customer stopped and glared at him but let him continue. "I am taking personal responsibility to make sure that your car is fixed right. Now, in order to solve your problem fast, I need to ask you a few questions. It will only take about two minutes, and it will save you time later. Is that all right with you?"

The Customer sighed deeply and then seemed to relax. Finally, someone was taking charge of this, so it was time to get on with it. "What do you need to know?" ❧

Of rough commands, and heated wrath
Reaction shunned and traction gained
I spring to action strong and fast
Divide the present from the past

❤ When action is demanded, make things happen fast.

Love Thy Customer

❤ Give pushy Customers time and encouragement to vent.

❤ State your positive intent when asking questions.

❤ When asking and answering questions, be direct and to the point.

❤ Establish that you are on the side of thy Customer.

CHAPTER 9

Temper Tantrums

When heat is hot, emotions flare
'Til clarity is brought to bear
I shall attend thee and show I care

"**I** have been an excellent Customer for over 10 years. I have always paid on time. You can look at my records."

"Blah, blah, blah," Marsha thought as she waited for the Customer to stop talking long enough to breathe. Then, when the opening came, she repeated for the third time, "Sir, I keep telling you, our policy is . . . " And that was as far as Marsha got.

The Customer seemed to snap. He completely lost it. Now he was ranting and raving, "No one cares. Nobody cares about anybody anymore! That's the problem with the world today."

"Sir, if you will just calm down!" Marsha demanded, disgusted by his irrational behavior.

"Calm down? Calm down?" He was getting louder by the second! "I can't believe it! Who the @#$#%^ does she think she's &^@#$ talking to?"

The slamming down of the phone was the last thing Marsha heard. "Sir? Sir?" she asked. "I guess he hung up," Marsha thought and then hoped that this particular call wasn't being monitored for quality assurance purposes. But then again, how could they fault her. Obviously, the guy was a nut case. ❧

Dealing with the Grenade

Your company works hard to provide a great service and excellent products. You personally go to great lengths to make sure that everybody gets served and served well. You'd think that would be enough, but is it? For some Customers, it's *never* enough! You know how it is. Out of nowhere, somebody starts losing it! Grenade behavior is a tantrum. The main reason why people lose control of themselves is that they feel undervalued and unappreciated. Then you may lose it because you feel unappreciated by them. Then your manager may lose it because she feels unappreciated by you. Then everyone takes it home to their families, where their spouses and kids feel unappreciated too. Next thing you know, the whole world is going crazy because of that one out-of-control Customer. But it doesn't have to be this way.

Although both the Tank and Grenade behaviors are intense to deal with, there are some important distinctions between the two that you must be able to make. A Tank attack is a demand for action. A Grenade tantrum is a demand for attention. Even while a Tank is attacking, you can gather information as to what her problem really is. When a Grenade explodes, nothing makes sense. His ranting and raving can be all over the map! With a Tank Customer, your goal is to move forward fast and make something happen. With a Grenade Customer, you usually have to stop everything and help him regain his self-control.

Don't let your Grenade Customer vent. Interrupt the tantrum by loudly saying the Customer's name a few times until you have his attention.

Blend by upping your energy. Show enthusiasm and energy for problem solving. Remember that a quiet and reasoned response to an excited and excitable person is like saying, "Want a little gas on your fire?" Remember, too, that it is impossible to reason with an emotional person. It is possible, though, to get an emotional person to become reasonable. Blend by increasing your energy, enthusiasm, and volume of your voice. You don't have to raise your voice to equal that of a Tank, but with a Grenade, you actually may have to speak louder than he just so that he can hear you.

Appreciate the Grenade Customer for something. Not for ruining your day, either! Instead, you can thank her for being honest about how she feels. You can appreciate her for taking the time to tell you. You can even thank her for giving you the opportunity to do something about it.

Love Thy Customer

Speak to the Grenade Customer's emotions with magical words such as, "I don't want you to feel that way!" and "I appreciate your business" and "That's terrible!" and "This is a misunderstanding!" Repeat these words over and over again until your out-of-control Grenade Customer starts to calm down.

Let your Grenade Customer follow you in for a soft landing. Never tell him to breathe or calm down. Instead, you breathe and you calm down. If you've done enough blending, he's sure to follow your lead. If an apology is in order, this would be a good time for it. "I'm really sorry! You shouldn't have been treated that way! The way you were dealt with is *not* acceptable!"

Call time out. If you are face to face and logistics permit, take the Grenade Customer to a new location so that she won't have to be embarrassed about having had a public tantrum. If you are on the phone, tell her that you have to look something up in her file and that you will call her back in just two minutes. Taking some kind of break after a tantrum is important because it gives the Grenade Customer a chance to regain composure. Ever had a Grenade Customer on the phone and you had to put him on hold and then pass him on to someone else in your organization? Typically, the next person to deal with him does not get a Grenade; she gets a nice, normal human being, because that little time out gave the Customer a chance to get control of himself again.

Tough Love

Pass along the person, but never pass along the problem behavior. Calling in a pinch hitter when someone loses control can be a great idea. You can tell your Grenade Customer, "We appreciate your business. And I want to make sure that you're talking to the best person to solve your problem." Then tell her who you're going to transfer her to and how long she is going to have to wait. There's nothing so maddening to a Grenade Customer as having to repeat a story about a problem that she never should have had in the first place. So tell the person you're transferring the Grenade Customer to all the facts of the situation. At this point, even the most agitated Grenade Customer will sense that you have her best interests in mind.

"I have been an excellent Customer of your company for over 10 years. I have always paid on time. You can look at my records."

"Blah, blah, blah," Marsha thought as she waited for the Customer to stop talking long enough to breathe. Then, when the opening came, she repeated for the third time, "Sir, I keep telling you, our policy is . . . " And that was as far as Marsha got.

The Customer seemed to snap. He completely lost it! Now he was ranting and raving, "No one cares. Nobody cares about anybody anymore! That's the problem with the world today!"

Suddenly Marsha realized that she had pulled the pin on a Grenade. She had just read about it in that Love Thy Customer book that management had bought for everyone to read. The word policy was probably a trigger, but feeling unappreciated was the cause. She suppressed the urge to tell him to calm down. Instead, she raised the volume of her voice a little and tried to say the words he needed to hear if he was ever to calm down. "Sir, Sir, Sir, I don't want you to feel that way! I care about you as a valuable Customer, and I assure you that we appreciate your business for the last 10 years. This is a misunderstanding, and I'm terribly sorry about this misunderstanding!" To her amazement, somewhere along the way, the Customer had stopped yelling. Marsha took a deep breath and continued to speak, and as she continued, she gradually brought her voice back down to a normal level and softened her tone. "I'm sure we can work this out, especially for a long-time Customer such as you." Marsha took another deep breath and heard her Customer follow her lead. "Let's just take a moment to collect our thoughts. I'm sure we can find a way to work this out." At this point Marsha's voice was as relaxed as if she were on a week's vacation. "In order to help you with this, I want to look something up in your file. Would you prefer that I call you back, or would you prefer to hold for about two minutes?"

"I'll hold," said the Customer.

A minute later, Marsha returned and found herself talking with a nice, calm Customer. She could hardly believe that this was the same person who had been yelling only a few minutes *earlier. She was able to resolve the situation to the Customer's satisfaction, and he thanked her three times before he got off the phone. Marsha had the thought, "I sure hope this call was monitored for quality assurance purposes" and chuckled to herself.* ❧

> When heat is hot, emotions flare
> 'Til clarity is brought to bear
> I shall attend thee and show I care

❤ Help thy Customer regain self-control by interrupting tantrums.

❤ Increase your energy level and raise the volume of your voice just a little.

❤ Say the words thy Customer needs to hear.

❤ Then lower your voice, soften your tone, and slow your breathing.

❤ Take some time out for thy Customer to regain composure.

CHAPTER 10

Knowledge
and the Lack Thereof

Should mouth be open and mind be closed
I bend my knee to not oppose
Both your manner and your prose

Lynn was the lead tech support for the premier image-editing program on the market. The new version had just come out, and the phone lines were jammed. They were now in that precarious situation where Customer problems needed to be solved, but calls had to be completed fast, or they'd be dealing with excessive hold times and hostile Customers. The current caller was a photographer who said that he was in a hurry, but apparently he had plenty of time to tell Lynn about his many years of experience with the software and all the famous people he had shot during those years. He dismissed her many attempts at helping him, claiming that he had already tried everything she suggested. She thought that she knew what he was doing that perpetuated his problem,

*but every time she tried to correct him, he would set her straight
on how much he knew and how little she knew in comparison.
His condescending attitude toward her was wearing thin, and it
seemed to Lynn that she was trapped in a call that had no end.
This caller was no doubt going to ruin her average handle time,
and as she watched the depth of the Q light go from green to yellow
to red, she felt a wave of hopelessness sweep over her.* ❧

Need to Know about the Ego

The difference between the Know-it-all and the Think-they-
know-it-all Customer is that the Know-it-all is knowledgeable
and, for the most part, knows what she's talking about. The
Think-they-know-it-all, on the other hand, does not know
what he is talking about but does not let that stop him from
talking. The Know-it-all Customer is a combination of Get It
Done and Get Appreciation. The Think-they-know-it-all
Customer has an intense need for attention and recognition.
If not knowledge, then what is the common denominator?
Both these behaviors represent people with a big ego.

Make such Customers feel important. You can say, "It's
great to talk to someone who understands these things!" and "I
guess I don't have to start with the usual ABC's with you!"

Gather information by backtracking and asking clarification questions. The Know-it-all Customer is happy to answer

questions because it lets him be the authority. And the Think-they-know-it-all Customer loves the attention.

Provide documentation whenever possible. By leading with statements such as, "Of course you've read about . . . " or "I'm sure you are aware of . . . ," you can then provide the documentation that makes your case in a nonthreatening way.

Be specific when problem solving. Make sure that the Customer has a sense of closure at every step by summarizing the problem, the findings, the next steps, and future options.

His *condescending attitude toward her was wearing thin. But then Lynn realized that she might make more progress if she went a little slower and blended with his huge ego.*

"Excuse me for interrupting," said Lynn respectfully. With the sound of excitement in her voice, she continued, "I just have to tell you how exciting it is to talk with an artist of your caliber. You are probably the most experienced photographer I have ever spoken to, and I am hoping you have a Web site so that I can see some of your work when we've completed this call."

"Well, of course I have a Web site! It's my name, jordan-jpetersen.com."

Lynn smiled to herself. Just what she expected. "Mr. Petersen, I plan to visit your site on my next break. Meanwhile, with all the work you do, I can only imagine how frustrating it must be to have to deal with the recent changes in the new ver-

sion of our software. Of course, I am certain you have seen a lot of changes since version 1.0. I started out with that version too, and as the lead tech support on this application, you can believe me when I tell you that I've heard more than a little frustration from valuable customers like yourself. Can you believe how much has changed since version 1.0? I'm curious, do you think the software has changed for the better?"

"Actually," Petersen replied, "I only started with this program at version 4.0, but I have to tell you what a pleasure it is to talk to someone like yourself who knows this software inside and out. I have spoken with a lot of tech supporters but never someone as knowledgeable as you."

Lynn couldn't believe it! One minute he was treating her as if she knew nothing, and now he was elevating her to an equal status. "Thank you. That means a lot coming from you, sir. If it's all right with you, I'd like to go over what you've done so far and help you resolve this problem so that you can get back to making art for the world to enjoy."

"Sounds good to me," said Petersen.

"Perhaps you have seen the knowledge base bulletin 53348? It's mentioned in the user documentation, but it's easy to miss. I'll highlight the important details with you, and then I'll also show you some tricks in the new software that will really impress your fellow photographers."

Tough Love

"I'd love that, thanks!" Petersen replied. "In fact, I can't wait!" 🌹

> Should mouth be open and mind be closed
> I bend my knee to not oppose
> Both your manner and your prose

💜 Feed the need of thy Customer's ego.

💜 Backtrack and clarify extensively to gather information.

💜 Refer to documentation to lead toward a solution.

💜 Make your case in a nonthreatening way.

💜 Create a sense of closure with every step forward.

CHAPTER 11

Helplessly Hoping

*Or hopeless now, thy whining great
My questions draw forth into light
And then remove the weight*

Janet had developed the habit of watching the ticks of the clock. On days like this, she hated her job and despised her Customers. Why couldn't they quit making excuses and just pay their credit-card bills? Who did they think was responsible for their sorry lives? There was still an hour to go before she could go home, and it felt like it would take forever.

How long had she been listening to this one? The customer was whining about her money problems and her relationship problems, and if Janet wasn't mistaken, she was telling her the same sad tale over and over again, like a broken record. Tick. Tock. "Oh puh-lease. Pa-the-tic." Janet often talked to herself as an alternative to listening to these sob stories.

Finally, Janet had enough. She cut the customer off and said, "Look our policy is to give you a few days, but you need to know that this is going to be on your credit report and . . . "

"My credit report?" whined the Customer. "But I have been sick and had to miss work and . . ."

"Oh no," thought Janet, "she is coming around for another pass. I've already heard all this!" Janet rubbed her temples as her head began to throb. Meanwhile, the Customer whined on. 🌹

The No Person, Whiner, and Nitpicker

No Person, Whiner, and Nitpicker Customers originate out of the intent to Get It Right. Details are important to some of your Customers, and the beginning of trouble is when details are discounted or missed. The result? Whenever it looks like things could be going wrong, Get It Right becomes a perfectionist. And then an unfunny thing happens on the way to customer service. Perfectionism yields to generalizations, Get It Right becomes It's Going Wrong, and behavior turns negative. Get It Right's words reflect the generalizations when telling you that "Nothing is right" and "Everything is wrong" because "Nobody cares," and "It's always like this."

Because negative generalizations can be time-consuming, you may think that you have to light a fire under these people to get them to move from problem finding to problem solving. But the problem is, if you try to push a "picky," "whiny," or "negative" Customer too hard, talk to her too fast, or cut her off from her concerns and complaints in order to straighten her out, she'll become even more nitpicking, whiny, and negative.

Your goal here is to turn a no-win situation into a no-lose situation, and here is how you do it: Pay attention to the details. Make sure that your conversational *t*'s are crossed and your *i*'s are dotted as a way of keeping any red flags from going up about the quality of service you hope to provide.

Backtrack and clarify. It may take patience and persistence to get to the bottom of the generalizations, so remember that generalizations are based on specifics. Don't expect your Customer to answer your questions right away. Sometimes he will replace one generalization with another. You say, "What's wrong?" And he says, "All of it." You say, "But what specifically is wrong?" And he says, "Everything." Do not give up. Just keep asking, and eventually you will get back to the specific details that led to the formation of the Customer's generalizations.

Ask open-ended questions to gather the highest-quality information. Open-ended questions begin with *who, what, where, when,* and *how.* Remember to repeat back what you've heard in order to make sure that you've got it right. This demonstrates to the Customer that your overriding concern is for nothing to go wrong.

When it is time for solutions, create a formal transition. After your detailed summary, ask, "Anything else? Do you feel that I understand the problem accurately?" If you can get a "Yes," then lead by presenting information step by logical step, and give the Customer the details. You may even want to set in place a mechanism to give the Customer regular progress reports. The best way to shift from problem finding to problem solving is to use some process to gather high-quality information and then to use that information in formulating a plan. Anything you can do to educate and empower your Customer on how to avoid problems in the future will be welcomed.

J*anet had another hour to go before she could go home. On the other end of the line was as sad a tale as you could imagine. On days like this, it sometimes seemed as if time were standing still, but Janet forced her attention away from the clock on the wall and just in time to notice that her Customer had begun repeating herself. Janet gently interrupted: "I'm sorry to interrupt you, Mrs. Jones, but I just want to make sure that I've understood what you're telling me." Janet then proceeded to backtrack what she had heard so far. As she did, it helped her clarify in her mind what questions she wanted to ask, and she wrote those questions down in between reading back what she had written while Mrs. Jones was speaking.*

She completed her summary, but before she could ask one of her questions, Mrs. Jones started in again. "It gets worse . . . " Oh well. At least Mrs. Jones wasn't repeating herself, so things must be going forward. Janet then summarized again, and this time she was able to ask her questions and get some answers, which she again summarized.

Now it was time to steer the conversation toward problem solving, "Mrs. Jones, I do understand that this is a hard time for you and your family, both emotionally and financially. Given the situation with your ex-husband, I'm sure that the last thing you want or need is a bad relationship with your bank. So let's consider what you can do to keep your accounts good with us. And I promise I'll be easier to talk to than your ex!"

At this Mrs. Jones laughed. "That's a relief! I guess I could pay this amount from my next paycheck, and then two weeks after that I could . . . " and Mrs. Jones began offering solutions.

Or hopeless now, thy whining great
My questions draw forth into light
And then remove the weight

💜 Don't push too hard or talk too fast. Take your time.

💜 Turn generalizations into specifics by backtracking and clarifying.

💜 Use open-ended questions that require more than a grunt.

❤ Create a formal transition from problem finding to problem solving.

❤ Set in place a mechanism for progress reports.

CHAPTER 12

Covert Operation

If words like arrows lack remorse
Then I remove them, seek the source

John *was just wrapping up the order with his Customer. "It looks like we'll get your order in before the 2:00 p.m. deadline," said John, "so this order should get to shipping today."*

"Yeah right, today. Uh-huh. Mmmm," said the Customer, with an unmistakable sound of sarcasm in his voice. It wasn't the first time during this call that the Customer had taken this tone.

"Oh well," John thought to himself. "No sense in making a big deal out of it."

"And, therefore, you should expect to see it by next Tuesday," he continued.

"Well, I certainly hope so. Tuesday, that would be lovely. I'd be very impressed," said the Customer, again with the same sarcasm.

John wondered if he should say something but then thought better of it. He completed the call and went on to the next Customer. ❧

Sniper Attack

Sniping takes many forms. It could be a cutting comment or a barb hidden in humor. It can be a sarcastic tone or a facial expression, such as the rolling of one's eyes. Whatever the form, its source is some kind of suppressed anger or resentment. It could relate to something happening right now or something that happened in the past. It could be something you said or didn't say or something your organization did or didn't do. Or it could be related to some other event or person in your Customer's life. But when a Customer snipes, it is wise to treat it as a demand for attention.

Call attention to the sniping. Do not ignore it. If it is a comment, backtrack it and then ask, "What's going on? Have I or my company offended you or let you down in some way?" More often than not the Sniping Customer will deflect this inquiry and say that it was nothing. Continue for one more round. "Are you sure, because if we did let you down, we certainly want to know about it. Your business is important to us." At this point, the Sniping Customer has two choices: Call off the attack or reveal its cause. If she chooses the former, go back to the business at hand of providing her with your loving service.

Show your Customer that you care. If she does reveal the reason she is upset, let her vent, offer statements of empathy, and backtrack and clarify until she confirms to you that she feels that you have completely understood.

Set things right. You may not be able to change the past, but perhaps you can provide something extra to make it up to your Customer. You also can take even more care in the present circumstances, giving your Customer your personal guarantee to watch over this so that it doesn't happen again.

John was just wrapping up the order with his Customer, Mrs. Swill. "It looks like we'll get your order in before the 2:00 p.m. deadline," said John, "so this order should get to shipping today."

"Yeah right, today. Uh-huh. Mmmm," said Mrs. Swill, with an unmistakeable sound of sarcasm in her voice. It wasn't the first time during this call that Mrs. Swill had taken this tone.

"Oh well," John thought to himself. "No sense in making a big deal out of it."

"And, therefore, you should expect to see it by next Tuesday," he continued.

"Well I certainly hope so. Tuesday, wouldn't that be a surprise!" said Mrs. Swill, again with the same sarcasm.

John then gently inquired, "Mrs. Swill, it sounds to me like there's something you're not saying. I'm wondering if I have done anything during this call or my company has done anything in the past that might be bothering you."

"No, no," said Mrs. Swill. "It's nothing, really."

Love Thy Customer

John pressed for more information, gently and with genuine caring. "You know, if there is something, I'd like to know what it is. If we let you down in some way, we need to know."

"Well . . . ," Mrs. Swill hesitated, "the last time I ordered from you, I made the 2:00 p.m. deadline, but my order didn't ship for two more days. And I told the Rep not to put a 'Signature Required' sticker on it. We live out in the country, and it is safe to leave a package on my front porch. But because of that sticker, I had to make a trip to the shipping location, a 40-minute drive, because I couldn't wait another day for it. So you lack a little credibility when you make promises, wouldn't you say?"

"Mrs. Swill, I am so sorry we inconvenienced you like that. It shouldn't have happened, and although I can't change the past, I can do something about the future. As soon as we get off the phone, I will personally contact the shipping department and make sure that this package goes out today, and with the 'No Signature Required' sticker."

"Why, thank you, young man," said Mrs. Swill. "It's my husband's birthday, and this is a gift for him. It would mean a lot to me if you got it right this time."

After John hung up the phone, he spoke to the manager of shipping, who thanked him for the feedback. They both made sure that the package was ready to go out the door that day and included a little birthday card from "the folks at shipping" and a 15 percent off coupon on the next order. 🌹

Tough Love

If words like arrows lack remorse
Then I remove them, seek the source

❤ Call attention to sarcasm by backtracking.

❤ Gently inquire in a caring fashion as to the source.

❤ If thy Customer says nothing is wrong, inquire again.

❤ Offer assurances of caring, interest, and desire for feedback.

❤ If the sarcasm stops, return to the business at hand.

❤ If thy Customer reveals a problem, empathize and set things right.

CHAPTER 13

Vague and Unresolved

Decisions made, yet still delayed
Some this, some that, and yet I serve
With gentle voice and plans to trade

After weeks of pursuing the client, Gary sat on a chair across the coffee table from the company's decision makers, Ned and Martha. He had just finished making his presentation. Ned and Martha looked at each other, nodded their heads, and turned and smiled at Gary. Gary, not afraid to close, popped the question: "I'd love to have your business. Are you ready to start the paperwork?"

Ned and Martha looked at each other, kind of nodded again, smiled, and Ned said, "You know it sounds real good."

"Yes it does," Martha added.

"Of course," continued Ned, "we really could use some time to think about it."

"Yes we could," added Martha enthusiastically.

"Are there any questions I can answer right now?" inquired Gary.

Ned and Martha both shrugged. Ned said, "I don't know."

"Yes," added Martha. "We need to think about that too."

Undeterred, Gary pressed ahead. "If there is one doubt that you have that would stop you from doing business with us, what would it be?"

"I don't know," said Ned.

"Let us think about it," Martha added. "And we'll get back to you." 🌹

Maybe People

Have you ever dealt with Customers who just couldn't make up their minds? Sometimes Customers occupy you with small talk and endless questions that seem to lead nowhere because there is something they're uncomfortable talking about. Their language may be vague and approximate. Maybe Customers put off a decision that could hurt someone's feelings, such as having to say "no" to a salesperson.

So create a Comfort Zone for them by showing your concern for their discomfort. Be nice enough to attend to their comfort while you gently gather some information. In this case, the quickest way to gather high-quality information is to slow down and speak in a considerate manner. With each reply to your request for information, check back with your Customers to make sure that you have understood them correctly.

Reassure your Customers that it is completely appropriate and, indeed, they are welcome to share problems and concerns with you. If you are in a sales position and you're facing a Maybe Customer who keeps putting off a decision while implying that it will be made soon, reassure him that it is okay to not do business with you, and it won't hurt your feelings. Let him know that it is good for you and good for him because you will get to move on to someone who could use your product or service. By doing this, you blend deeply with your Customer's desire to Get Along and relieve the pressure that stops him from telling you his true feelings.

Ironically, when you do this often, the Customer is so delighted at your sensitivity that he becomes more likely to buy from you. Or this might create enough comfort for him to voice his true concerns and give you a chance to respond to them. At this point of comfort, you can even walk your Customer through a decision-making process. Help him to think through each of his choices, one at a time, and consider both the positives and negatives.

After weeks of pursuing the client, Gary sat on a chair across the coffee table from the company's decision makers, Ned and Martha. He had just finished making his presentation. Ned and Martha looked at each other, nodded their heads, and turned and smiled at Gary. Gary, not afraid to close, popped the question: "I'd love to have your business. Are you ready to start the paperwork?"

Ned and Martha looked at each other, kind of nodded again, smiled, and Ned said, "Well, you know it sounds real good."

"Yes it does," Martha added.

"Of course," continued Ned, "we really could use some time to think about it."

"Yes we could," added Martha enthusiastically.

"I understand," Gary said. "This is an important decision. You have to make certain that you do what's best for your company. I respect that, and right now, more than anything else, that is what I want you to do. Even if your decision turns out to be no, it was still a pleasure meeting and talking with both of you."

Ned and Martha smiled and said, "It was nice to meet you, too."

"While you two discuss this, would you mind terribly if I used your facilities?" inquired Gary.

"Oh, please do," said Martha. "Up the hall, last door on the right."

"Thank you." Gary smiled and walked to the restroom. He didn't really need to rest, but he did want to give them time to talk without him present in the room. So he sat down, flipped through a magazine, and then washed his hands and returned.

Tough Love

Ned began, "We have discussed it, and we are ready to do the paperwork."

"Wonderful," said Gary. "You won't regret this. I know this is going to be the beginning of a beautiful relationship." 🌹

> Decisions made, yet still delayed
> Some this, some that, and yet I serve
> With gentle voice and plans to trade

❤ Create a comfort zone of concern for thy Customer's discomfort.

❤ Speak in a considerate and patient manner.

❤ Check back after each response to be certain you've heard correctly.

❤ Offer reassurances that sharing problems with you is appropriate.

❤ In a sales situation, reassure thy Customer that it is okay to say "no."

CHAPTER 14

All or Nothing

A paradox to find this sign
No words express thy feelings deep
I speak for thee, and thus reveal
The time is long, no moment cheap

"**H**ello, we're the Milo party," Pam said to the hostess. "We have a reservation at seven." It was their anniversary, and this was going to be a very special dinner.

"Welcome," said the hostess. "Yes, I have you down for two at 7:00 p.m., but we are running a bit behind. There was a theater event up the road, and everyone came in and ordered at the same time. But it shouldn't be long, maybe 10 minutes. Would you like to have a seat here or in the bar?"

It was Saturday night, and the bar was packed. There was no place to stand, let alone sit, except for a single seat near the hostess stand. So Pam sat while Blake stood. It was noisy and hard to carry on a conversation. Ten minutes came and went, then 15, and then 20. Finally, they were seated.

121

Love Thy Customer

When they called ahead, they were told the vegetarian special would be ratatouille, their favorite dish. It was what they had the night Blake had finally proposed. But on the list of daily specials, it was crossed off. However, a promise was prominently printed on the menu: "If you don't see what you want or have special needs, just ask, and we will do everything we can to accommodate you." So they asked about the ratatouille, and the waiter informed them that dish was unavailable. As Pam and Blake looked for another option, the waiter suddenly said, "I need to deliver some food. I'll be back," and he was gone.

Pam and Blake stared at each other. "Maybe coming here for our anniversary wasn't such a good idea after all!" said Pam.

"Let's make the most of it," replied Blake, although the disappointment in his voice was obvious. When the waiter returned, they placed an order. The food was nothing special. When the waiter rushed by their table, he asked, "Everything okay?"

Pam replied, "Yes, fine, thanks." But everything wasn't okay. The soup was so salty that Blake ate only a third of it. When they were nearly done with their entrees, they finally relaxed into a loving conversation with each other. That's when the waiter came by and asked, "Are you still working on that?" They looked at each other and decided they had had enough work for one evening. They skipped dessert and asked for the check. On the way out, the hostess asked, "How was everything?"

Pam and Blake smiled and nodded, opened the door, and left. As soon as they got outside, they resolved never to go back to that restaurant again. 🌹

Yes and Then Nothing

Yes and Nothing Customers operate under the axiom, "If you don't have something nice to say, then don't say anything at all." Some of the nicest people in the world have trouble talking about anything that might make waves, rock the boat, or cause problems for someone else. Yes Customers go along with you, but you don't really know what they feel or think. Nothing Customers simply say nothing, at least to the organization with whom they have a problem. Studies show that only 4 out of 100 people with a problem complain about it. If the problem is worth more than $100, 91 percent stop doing business with the offending organization and then tell their story to at least 9 other people.

If a Customer is not complaining, it may be tempting to leave well enough alone. After all, if the Customer is not making a big deal out of a problem, you might think that you're lucky and go about your business with no further concern. However, the Customer will have no problem talking to others about how bad your organization is or how poorly she was treated, thus costing you business, turning other Customers away from you. This is why you don't want to let Yes or Nothing Customers stay silent. The saying "Let sleeping dogs lie" may apply to dogs, but it's a poor guideline when it comes to doing business with people.

One way to get an honest conversation started is for you to say what your Customers are unwilling or unable to say. "This shouldn't have happened. We really let you down. If you will help me to understand this better, I'll do everything in my power to make it right and make it up to you." By talking to your Customers in this way, you signal that you care, and you are likely to win big with such Customers in the long run. In fact, instead of having them put down you or your organization to others, your sensitivity and attentiveness likely will turn them into evangelists for your company.

"**H**ello, we're the Milo party," Pam said to the hostess. "We have a reservation at seven." It was their anniversary, and it was going to be a very special dinner.

"Welcome" said the hostess. "Yes, I have you down for two at 7:00 p.m., but we are running a bit late. There was a theater event up the road, and everyone came in and ordered at the same time. But it shouldn't be long, maybe 10 minutes. Would you like to have a seat here or in the bar?"

It was Saturday night, and the bar was packed. There was no place to stand, let alone sit, except for a single seat near the hostess stand. So Pam sat while Blake stood. It was noisy and hard to carry on a conversation. Within a few minutes, though, the hostess came by and said that it was going to take a little longer than she had hoped. She offered a table in the bar where they could wait more comfortably. Pam said, "No, that's okay. We're fine here."

But the hostess insisted, "We know it's your anniversary, and you can't begin it standing around in here."

When they got to their table in the bar, two glasses of champagne were waiting for them. "Happy anniversary!" said the hostess cheerfully.

A little bit later they were shown to their table. When they had called ahead to reserve a table, they were told that the vegetarian special would be ratatouille, their favorite dish. It was what they had the night Blake had finally proposed. But on the list of daily specials, it was crossed off. However, a promise was prominently printed on the menu: "If you don't see what you want or have special needs, just ask, and we will do everything we can to accommodate you." So they asked about the ratatouille. The waiter empathized with their love for the dish, saying how much he loved it too. Unfortunately, he explained, key ingredients were out of season, but if they would share with him the flavors and textures they were interested in, he would talk to the chef.

The waiter came back with good news from the chef and also said that the manager wanted to buy them an appetizer to apologize for making them wait.

"Wow," said Pam and Blake to each other. The meal was great, except for the soup, which was so salty that Blake could only eat a third of it. As they neared the end of their entree, the waiter came by, waited patiently for them to notice him (they were lost in romantic conversation at that point), and asked if they were still enjoying their meal or should he take it away. They looked at each other and realized how stupid the expression is that most waiters use, "Are you still working on it?" This waiter apparently understood that a meal out should be pleasure, not work. They marveled at how attentive to every detail everyone had been, right down to the question, "Are you still enjoying your meal?"

When they got their check, the waiter noted that he didn't charge them for the soup. "After all, it didn't seem like you enjoyed it."

When they were on the way out, the hostess apologized again for their having to wait for a table and wished them a happy anniversary.

Pam and Blake smiled and said, "Thank you, it was wonderful."

The moment they were outside, they looked at each other, and Blake exclaimed, "Your father's retirement dinner? Let's do it here!" Then they strolled down the street, arm in arm, smiling at their good fortune. ❧

Tough Love

A paradox to find this sign
No words express thy feelings deep
I speak for thee, and thus reveal
The time is long, no moment cheap

❤ Lack of complaints does not mean everything is okay.

❤ When things go wrong, say what thy Customer is unable to say.

❤ Though nothing is demanded, make it right.

Your Service Matters

Relationship's a fickle thing
So I love thee as I love myself
A golden rule for truth to tell
'Tis you I live to serve so well

The principle of love is that you win when others win. When we help each other out, our load is made lighter, and our lives are made easier. If we look out only for ourselves, however, the center of the relationship does not hold, and things fall apart. Don't take our word for it. Pay attention, and you'll discover that if what we say is true, then life's true meaning will be discovered in the powerful side effects of loving service to others.

Your service matters. Never doubt it. And not in some generic way but in a specific way that only you can know. The meaning of your service presents itself to you through those unexpected and surprising moments of clarity when you experience the reality that someone's life is made better as a result of something you've said or done.

Love Thy Customer

Believe it or not, there are people who spend their lives giving service and never recognizing what it is they do. They do what they're told, they try not to give it too much attention, and then they go home and try to forget about it. Your life doesn't have to be that way. You, dear reader, deserve a better life than that. And you can have it. Just remember to Love Thy Customer, and Thy Customer's Love will return to you multiplied.

Relationship's a fickle thing
So I love thee as I love myself
A golden rule for truth to tell
'Tis you I live to serve so well

Invitation from
the Authors

If you would like to learn more about our other books and audio and video, programs, visit the following Web sites:

www.LoveThyCustomers.com

www.DealingWithRelatives.com

www.DealingWithPeople.com

The authors can be reached by e-mail at

Dr. Rick Kirschner: *dr.rick@talknatural.com*

Dr. Rick Brinkman: *dr.rick@rickbrinkman.com*

About the Authors

Dr. Rick Kirschner and Dr. Rick Brinkman are world-renowned professional speakers and trainers. They are the coauthors of the bestselling audio- and videotape series *How to Deal with Difficult People* and have authored six other audio and video training programs. Their book *Dealing with People You Can't Stand* is an international bestseller, now available in a revised second edition with translations in 15 languages. They wrote the entertaining and practical sequel *Dealing with Relatives: Your Guide to Successful Family Relationships* and they coauthored the book *Life by Design, Making Wise Choices in a Mixed Up World*. They now present their entertaining keynote speeches and training programs worldwide. Their client portfolio includes AT&T, Hewlett-Packard, the Inc. 500 Conference, Young Presidents Organization, the U.S. Army, and hundreds of other corporations, government agencies, medical conferences, educational groups, and professional associations.

For information about Dr. Kirschner's keynotes and seminars, visit *www.QuickChangeArtist.com*. For information about Dr. Brinkman's keynotes and seminars, visit *www.RickBrinkman.com*. To learn more about their work together, visit *www.TheRicks.com*.